Salad Masterclass

1500 Days of Colorful and Creative Recipes to Master the Art of Salad Making | Full Color Edition

Laura K. Cuadra

Editor: Aaliyah Lyons
Cover Art: Danielle Rees
Interior Design: Brooke White
Food stylist: Sienna Adams

TABLE OF CONTENTS

Introduction 1

CHAPTER 1: **The Artistry of Salad-Making** 2

The Foundation of Salad-Making 2

Newbie's Salad Toolkit 2

Seasonal Sensations 4

CHAPTER 2: **Flavorful Dressings** 6

Dill, Lemon, and Garlic Sour Cream Dressing................................. 7

Cilantro-Lime Dressing 7

Cumin-Mint Yogurt Dressing 8

Red Hot Chilli Dip 8

Sweet & Spicy Tomato Pasta Sauce 9

Mango Avocado Dressing.. 9

Avocado-Yogurt Dressing 10

Raspberry Vinaigrette.. 10

Honey Spice Vinaigrette 11

Asian Soy Vinaigrette 11

CHAPTER 3: **Vibrant Vegetable Salads and Slaws** 12

Red Cabbage and Apple Salad... 13

Crispy Fried Brussels Sprouts Salad 13

Italian Potato Salad 14

Spring Breakfast Salad... 14

Zoodle Greek Salad 15

Pesto–Raw Kale Salad 15

Fennel Salad 16

Sweet & Sour Cucumber Salad 16

Creamy Elote Salad 17

Radish, Cucumber, Lox, and Dill Salad... 17

Fall Salad... 18

Raw Carrot & Date Walnut Salad 18

Carrot Beet Apple Slaw 19

Warm Sweet Potato & Brussels Sprout Salad 19

CHAPTER 4: **Wholesome Grain, Bean, and Pasta Salads** 20

Calabrian Green Bean Salad 21

White Bean Tomato Salad 21

Black Bean and Orange Salad.. 22

Zesty Lemon Orzo Pasta Salad... 22

Elegant Brunch Snap Peas and Soft-Boiled Egg 23

Mixed Bean and Pumpkin Salad... 23

Balela Salad 24

Italian Bean and Rice Salad 24

Rice Noodle Salad with Orange and Edamame...................................... 25

Snap Pea Broccoli Slaw 25

Charred Poblano, Corn, and Wild Rice Salad... 26

CHAPTER 5: Tasty Tofu and Egg Salads 27

Spinach Salad with Poached Eggs and Bacon....................................... 28

Avocado and Bacon Egg Salad 28

Asian Sesame Tofu Salad 29

Greek Tofu Salad 29

Curry Egg Salad... 30

Tofu and Avocado Salad 30

Mango and Tofu Summer Salad 31

Classic Egg Salad 31

Spinach Egg Salad with Dijon Vinaigrette... 32

Creamy Avocado Egg Salad.. 32

Caprese Egg Salad 33

Warm Bell Pepper and Tofu Salad 33

CHAPTER 6: Fresh Fish and Seafood Salads 34

Pineapple Coconut Shrimp Salad 35

Creamy Tuna and Cabbage Salad 35

Shaved Brussels Sprout and Shrimp Salad 36

Tuna Salad with Lime Mayo.. 36

French Salmon Salad... 37

Tuna Salad Wraps.. 37

Tuna Niçoise Salad 38

Seafood Quinoa Salad with Lemon-Dill Vinaigrette.............................. 39

Crab Salad with Baby Asparagus.. 40

Shrimp and Cauliflower Salad with Dill Dressing................................... 40

Creamy Oysters Salad 41

Beachy Cold Shrimp Corn Salad... 41

Cajun Shrimp Salad... 42

Salmon Salad Cups.. 42

CHAPTER 7: Scrumptious Chicken Salads..**43**

Cajun Lime Avocado Chicken Salad 44

Old-Fashioned Chicken Salad.. 44

Chicken Gyro Salad 45

Mom's Chicken Salad 45

Pear, Pecan, and Chicken Salad.. 46

Apple, Walnut, and Chicken Salad... 46

Roasted Vegetable and Chicken Salad 47

Grilled Chicken Salad.. 47

Thai Chicken and Peanut Salad 48

Asparagus Chicken Salad 49

Minty Green Chicken Salad 49

Pineapple, Cashew, and Chicken Salad.. 50

Mango Avocado Chicken Salad 50

Strawberry and Chicken Salad.. 51

Mango, Avocado, and Chicken Salad 52

CHAPTER 8: Savory Meat Salads **53**

Fennel, Seared Pork, and Pineapple Salad 54

Asian-Style Steak Salad 54

Lamb and Greek Salad 55

Easy Steak Salad 55

BBQ Chicken and Corn Salad.. 56

Thai Beef Salad 56

Stuffed Pork with Red Cabbage Salad 57

Taco Salad.. 57

Warm Rump Steak Salad 58

Smoked Salmon and Asparagus Salad 58

Thai Pork Salad 59

Turkey and Cranberry Quinoa Salad 60

Beef and Feta Salad 60

Grilled Steak and Blue Cheese Salad 61

Grilled Lamb and Mediterranean Couscous Salad.................................... 61

Beef and Avocado Quinoa Salad... 62

APPENDIX 1: Measurement Conversion Chart **63**

APPENDIX 2: The Dirty Dozen and Clean Fifteen..............................**64**

APPENDIX 3: Index..**65**

INTRODUCTION

In the realm of culinary creativity, where flavors harmonize and colors dance, I invite you to explore a culinary experience like no other. The pages you hold in your hands are not just a collection of recipes but a gateway to a world where salads transcend their stereotype and emerge as culinary masterpieces.

Picture yourself navigating through a garden of vibrant greens, crisp vegetables, and an array of textures that promise to awaken your palate. In Salad Masterclass, we delve into the heart of salad-making, unraveling the artistry that transforms a humble bowl of greens into a symphony of tastes and sensations.

In a world that often glorifies intricate dishes, salads stand as a testament to simplicity's power—a canvas for culinary expression where health and flavor coalesce. This isn't a rulebook but an invitation to explore, experiment, and savor the joy of creating meals that nourish both body and soul.

Discover the alchemy of crafting the perfect dressing, understand the delicate balance that elevates a salad from ordinary to extraordinary, and embrace the freedom to mix and match ingredients that resonate with your unique taste. Salad Masterclass is an ode to the endless possibilities that unfold when fresh, wholesome ingredients are brought together with intention and imagination.

From refreshing summer salads to hearty winter bowls, each recipe is a chapter in the saga of exploring the boundless potential inherent in a bowl of greens. So, set forth on this gastronomic journey, let your taste buds be your guide, and redefine your understanding of salads—one delectable creation at a time.

May this book inspire you to celebrate the culinary marvel that is the salad, where simplicity meets sophistication, and each bite is an invitation to savor the extraordinary in the ordinary. Bon appétit!

Chapter 1: The Artistry of Salad-Making

The Foundation of Salad-Making

Exploring Greens

The bedrock of any exceptional salad lies in the selection of greens. While iceberg lettuce and spinach are commonly known, the world of greens extends far beyond these staples. Consider experimenting with a variety of leafy greens such as arugula, watercress, and radicchio. Each green brings its own unique flavor profile and texture to the table. Arugula, for example, introduces a peppery kick, while watercress contributes a slightly bitter note. By combining different greens, you create a dynamic base that adds complexity to your salad.

Moreover, don't shy away from venturing beyond traditional leafy greens. Kale, with its robust texture, offers a hearty foundation, and mixed microgreens provide a delicate, nuanced touch. Remember that a well-balanced salad often features a blend of textures, so consider combining softer greens with crunchier options like romaine or endive. This variety not only enhances the eating experience but also maximizes nutritional diversity.

Crafting the Perfect Dressing

The dressing serves as the flavor conductor in the symphony of a salad. Crafting the perfect dressing involves striking a harmonious balance between acidity, sweetness, and richness. Start with a classic vinaigrette as a versatile base. A simple recipe includes extra-virgin olive oil, balsamic vinegar, Dijon mustard, honey, and a pinch of salt and pepper. Experiment with different types of vinegar—red wine, apple cider, or champagne vinegar—to tailor the acidity to your liking.

Consider incorporating fresh herbs, minced garlic, or citrus zest to elevate the dressing's complexity. Whisking or shaking the ingredients vigorously helps emulsify the dressing, ensuring a smooth, well-blended texture. Remember that the key to a great dressing is not only the ingredients but also the ratio. Tasting and adjusting as you go is the secret to finding the perfect balance that complements your chosen greens and toppings.

Balancing Flavors and Textures

A successful salad is a sensory adventure, and achieving the right balance of flavors and textures is paramount. Begin by considering the flavor profiles of your chosen greens. Peppery arugula may pair well with sweet fruits like strawberries, while the bitterness of radicchio can be balanced with the sweetness of roasted beets.

Introduce a variety of textures to keep each bite interesting. Crisp cucumbers, juicy cherry tomatoes, and creamy avocados add layers of sensation. Nuts, seeds, or croutons contribute a satisfying crunch, while cheese provides a luxurious creaminess. When planning your salad, envision a symphony of tastes and textures—create harmony by ensuring no single element dominates.

Newbie's Salad Toolkit

Embarking on a journey into salad making as a newbie requires a set of tools that are not only fundamental but also make the process efficient and enjoyable. Here's a comprehensive guide to some essential salad making tools and preparations that will equip you for success in the kitchen:

· **Quality Cutting Board and Sharp Knife:**
■ Invest in a sturdy cutting board to provide a stable surface for chopping vegetables and greens.
■ A sharp chef's knife is a kitchen essential for precise and efficient cutting. It ensures clean, uniform slices and reduces the risk of accidents.

· **Salad Spinner:**
■ A salad spinner is a game-changer for washing and drying greens. It helps remove excess water, ensuring that your salad ingredients stay crisp and the dressing adheres well.

· **Vegetable Peeler:**
■ A good vegetable peeler is handy for peeling and thinly slicing vegetables. It adds a professional touch to your salads and allows for creative presentations.

· **Mandoline Slicer:**
■ While not essential, a mandoline slicer can be a time-saving tool for achieving consistent, thin slices of vegetables. It's particularly useful for ingredients like cucumbers and radishes.

· **Mixing Bowls:**
■ Have an assortment of mixing bowls in various sizes. They are versatile for tossing salads, preparing dressings, and organizing ingredients. Opt for bowls made of durable materials like stainless steel or glass.

· **Whisk or Dressing Shaker:**
■ A reliable whisk or a dressing shaker is essential for emulsifying salad dressings. Choose one that is easy to clean and allows you to create well-blended dressings for your salads.

· **Tongs and Salad Servers:**
■ Tongs provide an efficient way to toss salads without damaging delicate ingredients. Invest in a pair with a good grip.
■ Salad servers, whether wooden or stainless steel, are handy for serving salads elegantly.

· **Grater or Zester:**
■ A grater or zester adds texture to your salads by allowing you to incorporate citrus zest, cheese, or finely grated vegetables. It's a small tool that can make a big difference in flavor.

· **Garlic Press:**
■ For those who enjoy the robust flavor of garlic in their dressings, a garlic press simplifies the process and ensures that the garlic is evenly distributed.

· **Measuring Cups and Spoons:**
■ Achieving the right balance of ingredients is crucial. Measuring cups and spoons are essential for accurately portioning items like dressings, oils, and vinegar.

· **Storage Containers:**
■ Prepare your salads in advance and keep them fresh by storing components in airtight containers. This is particularly helpful for meal prepping or taking salads on the go.

· **Herb Scissors or Kitchen Shears:**
■ To effortlessly chop herbs, invest in herb scissors or kitchen shears. They provide a quick and efficient way to add freshness to your salads.

· **Salad Bowl:**
■ Having a dedicated salad bowl, preferably a large and attractive one for serving, adds a touch of presentation to your culinary creations.

· **Digital Kitchen Scale:**

■ For precise measurements, especially when following specific recipes, a digital kitchen scale is a useful tool. It ensures accuracy in portion control and ingredient quantities.

· **Salad Recipe Inspirations:**

■ Lastly, arm yourself with a variety of salad recipes to inspire your culinary creativity. Explore different flavor profiles, ingredient combinations, and techniques to keep your salads exciting and diverse.

Seasonal Sensations
Crafting Salads for Every Season

Salads are a dynamic canvas that evolves with the changing seasons, offering a culinary experience that aligns with nature's rhythm. Crafting salads tailored to each season allows you to celebrate the unique flavors and textures that come to life during specific times of the year.

● *Spring:* As the world awakens from winter slumber, embrace the freshness of spring in your salads. Incorporate tender asparagus, crisp radishes, and vibrant peas for a burst of green vitality. Pair these seasonal gems with lighter greens like spinach or butter lettuce, creating salads that reflect the rejuvenation of the season. Consider a zesty lemon vinaigrette to complement the delicate flavors of spring.

● *Summer:* The abundance of summer brings forth a kaleidoscope of colors and bold, juicy flavors. Create refreshing salads with heirloom tomatoes, sweet corn, and ripe berries. Incorporate herbs like basil and mint for a cooling effect. Grilled vegetables and proteins add a smoky depth, making summer salads a delightful medley of tastes and textures.

● *Fall:* Transition into fall with salads that capture the warmth and earthiness of the season. Roasted butternut squash, crisp apples, and hearty grains like farro or barley create a comforting foundation. Earthy greens such as kale or arugula pair well with autumnal ingredients. Consider drizzling a maple or balsamic glaze for a touch of sweetness that resonates with the season.

- *Winter:* Embrace the heartiness of winter with salads that provide both warmth and nourishment. Roasted Brussels sprouts, sweet potatoes, and citrus fruits add vibrancy to your winter creations. Include grains like quinoa or couscous for a satisfying base. A pomegranate vinaigrette or a citrus-infused dressing can bring a refreshing contrast to the richer, roasted elements.

Embracing Seasonal Produce for Optimal Freshness

The key to an exceptional seasonal salad lies in embracing the abundance of fresh, locally sourced produce. Optimal freshness enhances the flavors, textures, and nutritional value of your salads.

Farmers' Markets: Explore local farmers' markets to discover a treasure trove of seasonal produce. Engage with farmers to learn about the freshest picks of the season and incorporate them into your salads. This not only ensures premium quality but also supports local agriculture.

Understanding Seasonal Cycles: Familiarize yourself with the natural growing cycles of fruits and vegetables in your region. This knowledge allows you to anticipate and celebrate the arrival of specific ingredients, optimizing their use when they are at their peak.

Adaptability: While certain ingredients are associated with specific seasons, adaptability is key. Experiment with variations of a salad based on the availability of produce. Substituting similar seasonal ingredients ensures that your salads remain fresh and exciting throughout the year.

Preservation Techniques: Extend the lifespan of seasonal produce by exploring preservation techniques. Pickling, fermenting, or even freezing can help you enjoy the flavors of a particular season beyond its peak. This enables you to incorporate your favorite seasonal elements into salads throughout the year.

In conclusion, mastering the art of salad-making transcends the mere assembly of ingredients; it is a journey of creativity, exploration, and culinary joy. As we've delved into the foundational elements, ingredient pairings, seasonal inspirations, and essential tools, envision salads not just as dishes but as vibrant expressions of your culinary prowess. The balance of flavors, the dance of textures, and the harmony of ingredients are your tools to orchestrate a symphony on the plate.

Whether you are a seasoned chef or a novice in the kitchen, the world of salads beckons with endless possibilities. Let your imagination run wild as you experiment with diverse greens, flavors, and seasonal produce. Embrace the simplicity of a well-crafted vinaigrette and revel in the transformative power of ingredient pairings.

As you embark on your salad-making adventure armed with newfound knowledge and essential tools, savor the process. Let each salad be a reflection of your personal taste and a celebration of the culinary artist within you. with the right foundation and a dash of inspiration, you are poised to create salads that not only nourish the body but also delight the senses. May your culinary journey be filled with creativity, delicious discoveries, and a bounty of vibrant salads.

Chapter 2:

Flavorful Dressings

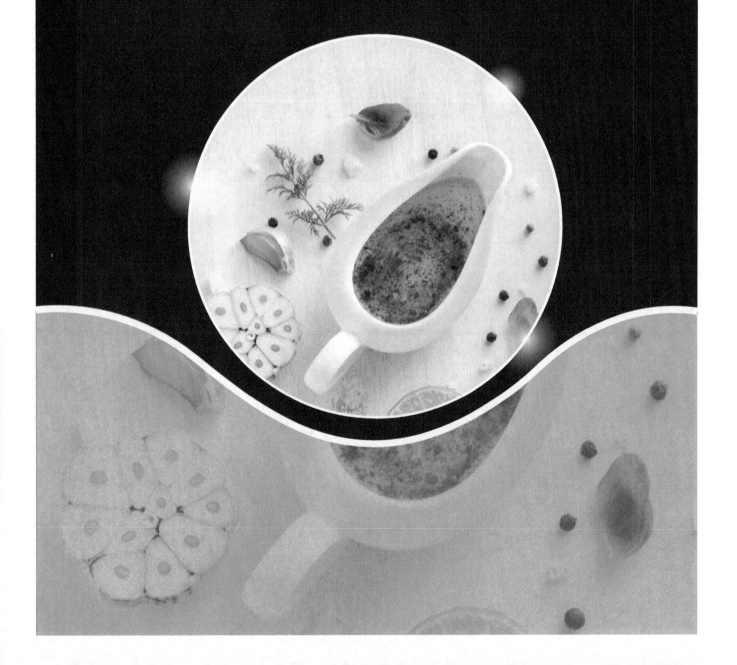

Dill, Lemon, and Garlic Sour Cream Dressing

Necessary products
1 cup full-fat sour cream
¼ cup loosely packed dill sprigs
Juice of 1 lemon
1 small garlic clove, minced
Pinch salt
Pinch freshly ground black pepper

Preparation
1. Add the ingredients to a small bowl, Mason jar, or salad dressing shaker. Whisk to combine, or shake the bottle.
2. Seal the container and refrigerate for up to 5 days. The dressing is at its best about 4 hours after making, once the flavors have melded together.

Cilantro-Lime Dressing

Necessary products
¾ cup grapeseed oil
¼ cup high-quality extra-virgin olive oil
Grated zest of 2 limes
Juice of 2 limes
¼ cup loosely packed fresh cilantro leaves
Pinch salt
Pinch freshly ground black pepper

Preparation
1. Add the ingredients to a small bowl, Mason jar, or salad dressing shaker.
2. Whisk to combine, or shake the bottle. This dressing will last up to 2 weeks at room temperature. Give it a shake before dressing a salad with it.

Cumin-Mint Yogurt Dressing

Prep time: 5 minutes | Cook time: none | Serves 4

Necessary products

1 cup full-fat plain Greek yogurt
1 teaspoon ground cumin
Grated zest of ½ small lemon
Juice of ½ small lemon
¼ cup loosely packed fresh mint leaves
1 small garlic clove, minced
Pinch salt
Pinch freshly ground black pepper

Preparation

1. Place all the ingredients in a blender. Blend until completely smooth. Taste and adjust the seasonings as needed. If the dressing is too thick, blend in a few tablespoons of water or more lemon juice.
2. Transfer to a resealable container, Mason jar, or dressing shaker and refrigerate for up to 4 days.

Red Hot Chilli Dip

Prep time: 10 minutes | Cook time: none | Serves 4

Necessary products

1 cup raw cashews soaked and drained
1/2 cup sun dried tomatoes (reserve the water just in case)
1 red capsicum (red bell pepper) seeded
1/2 red chilli (deseeded and chopped) leave it out if you want a mild dip
1/4 cup olive oil
Sea salt and pepper to taste

Preparation

1. Blend all ingredients until smooth adding the oil little by little to get the desired consistency.
2. Add as much chilli as you like (with or without the seeds).

Sweet & Spicy Tomato Pasta Sauce

Prep time: 5 minutes | Cook time: none | Serves 4

Necessary products
1 cup "Homemade Semi-Dried Tomatoes" (or
    2/3 cup store-bought dried toms) soaked
    one hour, keep the water
2 soft dates, pitted
2 cloves garlic, chopped
2 big or 3 medium tomatoes
1 tsp dried oregano
1/4 cup fresh basil, shredded
4 tbsp cold pressed olive oil
2 tbsp fresh lemon juice
A pinch of cayenne or 1 teaspoon sweet paprika

Preparation
1. Blend all ingredients in a machine to get
    desired consistency.
2. Make your adjustments including adding
    the soak water as you need it.

Mango Avocado Dressing

Prep time: 5 minutes | Cook time: none | Serves 4

Necessary products
1 large mango, flesh
2 medium avocados, flesh only (or 1 large)
1 clove garlic, minced
Grate the zest of a lemon, to get ½ - 1 tsp for
    your dressing ... then
1 lemon, juiced
1 small jalapeño (or other chilli pepper), seeded
    (keep seeds to increase heat)
2 tbsp honey or agave nectar
2 tbsp cold pressed olive oil
1 tsp apple cider vinegar

Preparation
1. Place all ingredients in a blender and
    process until smooth. This may be thick.
2. Add water or coconut water to thin until
    desired consistency is achieved.

Avocado-Yogurt Dressing

Prep time: 5 minutes | Cook time: none | Serves 4

Necessary products

1 large, ripe avocado, pitted
½ cup plain Greek yogurt
¼ cup loosely packed cilantro leaves
¼ cup loosely packed parsley leaves
Grated zest of 1 lime
Juice of 1 lime
1 small garlic clove
Pinch salt
Pinch freshly ground black pepper

Preparation

1. Place all the ingredients in a blender. Blend until completely smooth. Taste and adjust the seasonings as needed.
2. Transfer to a resealable container, Mason jar, or dressing shaker. The dressing can be refrigerated for up to 2 days, but it is best if eaten right away.

Raspberry Vinaigrette

Prep time: 5 minutes | Cook time: none | Serves 4

Necessary products

1/4 cup raspberries
3+ tbsp orange juice
2 tbsp olive oil
1/2 tbsp lemon juice
Sea salt and pepper to taste

Preparation

1. Blend all ingredients in a blender until smooth. Check the flavor and adjust. It may need more salt than you initially consider to get the balance right. Variability of produce is always an element here and in many dressings so be willing to adjust to create balance of the sweet, salt, and sour.
2. You may choose to pass the vinaigrette through a sieve to remove any seeds.

Honey Spice Vinaigrette

Necessary products
1/4 cup olive, walnut or hazelnut oil
1 tbsp red wine vinegar
1/4 tsp sea salt
A good grinding of fresh pepper
1/4 tsp cinnamon
1/4 tsp cumin
1 tsp honey

Preparation
1. Whisk all the dressing ingredients except the oil. Then add the oil to emulsify the dressing.
2. Adjust your dressing (with honey, salt, spice or vinegar). Combine with the salad ingredients and serve.

Asian Soy Vinaigrette

Necessary products
1 cup low-sodium soy sauce
3 tablespoons sesame oil
1 tablespoon honey
1 (1-inch) piece fresh ginger, grated
¼ teaspoon grated orange zest
¼ teaspoon grated lime zest
½ tablespoon minced chives or scallions
Small handful fresh cilantro leaves
Pinch salt
Pinch freshly ground black pepper
Togarashi seasoning (optional, for additional heat and spice)

Preparation
1. Add the ingredients to a small bowl, Mason jar, or salad dressing shaker.
2. Whisk to combine, or shake the bottle. This dressing will last up to 2 weeks at room temperature. Give it a shake before dressing a salad with it.

Chapter 3:

Vibrant Vegetable Salads and Slaws

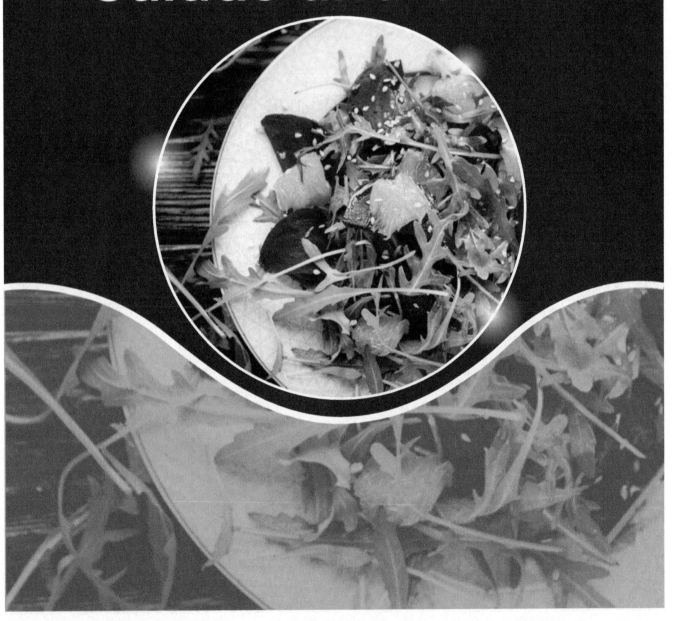

Red Cabbage and Apple Salad

Prep time: 10 minutes | Cook time: none | Serves 4

Necessary products

1 head red cabbage, quartered, cored, and
   sliced thinly
1 carrot, peeled and grated
2 apples, cored and diced
3 tablespoons olive oil
3 tablespoons apple cider vinegar
Salt and pepper to taste
½ cup almonds, slivered or chopped and
   toasted

Preparation

1. Combine the cabbage, carrot, and apple
   pieces in a bowl and mix well.
2. Make the dressing by whisking together
   the olive oil and apple cider vinegar.
3. Drizzle the dressing over the salad, mix
   well, taste, and add salt and pepper as
   desired.
4. Garnish with the almonds.

Crispy Fried Brussels Sprouts Salad

Prep time: 10 minutes | Cook time: 10 minutes | Serves 4

Necessary products

3 tablespoons canola oil
2 (9-ounce) bags shaved Brussels sprouts
2 cups shredded red cabbage
1 cup crispy onions
Sweet Chili Dressing
2 tablespoons sweet chili sauce
2 tablespoons vegetable oil
1 tablespoon freshly squeezed lime juice
1 teaspoon soy sauce

Preparation

1. In a small bowl, whisk all the ingredients
   together. Taste for seasoning. Store any
   leftover dressing in an airtight container in
   the refrigerator for up to 1 week.
2. In a large nonstick pan, heat the oil over
   high heat.
3. Add the Brussels sprouts and fry for 8 to
   10 minutes, until the edges become crispy
   and golden brown. Remove the Brussels
   sprouts from the pan and set aside on
   paper towels to remove excess oil.
4. In a large bowl, toss the Brussels sprouts, red cabbage, and crispy onions with 2
   tablespoons of Sweet Chili Dressing. Taste and add more dressing, if desired.

Italian Potato Salad

Necessary products
1 tablespoon salt
1½ pounds red potatoes (about 6),
peeled and cut into bite-sized pieces
3 tablespoons olive oil
2 garlic cloves, peeled and minced
3 tablespoons chopped chives
¼ teaspoon crushed red pepper
¼ cup chopped parsley
Salt and pepper to taste

Preparation
1. Add the salt to a large pot of water
   (at least 2 quarts), add the potatoes and bring to a boil.
2. Boil the potatoes for approximately 10-12 minutes, until a sharp knife inserted into a
   large piece of potato goes in and comes out with very little resistance (or take a piece
   out and see if it smashes easily with a fork). Drain but don't rinse the potatoes and place
   them in a bowl.
3. Make the dressing by whisking together the olive oil, minced garlic, chives, crushed red
   pepper, and chopped parsley.
4. Drizzle the dressing over the potatoes, mix well, taste, and add salt and pepper as
   desired.

Spring Breakfast Salad

Necessary products
½ cup strawberries
½ cup blueberries
½ cup blackberries
½ cup raspberries
1 grapefruit, peeled and segmented
3 tablespoons fresh orange juice (from 1 orange)
1 tablespoon pure maple syrup
¼ cup chopped fresh mint
¼ cup sliced almonds

Preparation
1. In a serving bowl, combine the berries and
   grapefruit.
2. In a small bowl, stir together the orange juice
   and maple syrup. Pour the syrup mixture over
   the fruit. Sprinkle with the mint and almonds.
   Serve immediately.

Zoodle Greek Salad

Prep time: 20 minutes | Cook time: 5 minutes | Serves 2

Necessary products
2 large zucchinis
1¼ cups cherry tomatoes, halved
2 Persian cucumbers, halved lengthwise and
    cut into half-moons
½ cup pitted Kalamata olives or other assorted
    pitted olives, halved
¼ cup Lemon Vinaigrette
Salt
Freshly ground black pepper
½ cup crumbled feta cheese

Preparation
1. Spiralize the zucchini into noodles (or zoodles), leaving the skin on. Alternatively, use a vegetable peeler to shave the zucchini into thin strips.
2. Combine the zucchini, tomatoes, cucumbers, and olives in a large bowl. Drizzle with the vinaigrette and toss to combine. Season with salt and pepper.
3. Divide the salad between two plates or bowls. Garnish with the feta and serve cold.

Pesto-Raw Kale Salad

Prep time: 10 minutes | Cook time: 15 minutes | Serves 4

Necessary products
1 bunch kale, stems removed and thinly
    sliced into ribbons
2 tablespoons extra-virgin olive oil
3 tablespoons fresh lemon juice
sea salt and ground black pepper
For Topping:
4 tablespoons basil pesto
1 ripe avocado, diced
½ cup savory granola (below)

Preparation
1. Place the kale in a large serving bowl and drizzle it with the oil. With clean hands, gently massage the kale and oil for 5 minutes, or until the kale is tenderized. Pour the lemon juice over the top and season well with salt and pepper to taste.
2. Divide the kale among 4 plates. Top each with a heaping tablespoon of pesto, some diced avocado, and 2 tablespoons granola. Serve immediately.

Fennel Salad

Prep time: 10 minutes | Cook time: none | Serves 4

Necessary products
1.5 cup fennel bulb, finely sliced
1 large green apple, (julienned) cut into match sticks or thin slices
1 cup mixed greens or arugula (rocket)
1 tbsp fresh finely chopped thyme (or tarragon)
Optional: 1 tbsp chilli pepper, seeded and finely minced or some cayenne or paprika

Preparation
1. Combine all ingredients together.
2. If you have to prepare this before you are ready to eat, then add some dressing or plain lemon juice to the apple to prevent it going brown.

Sweet & Sour Cucumber Salad

Prep time: 5 minutes | Cook time: none | Serves 4

Necessary products
Salad
Finely slice your cucumber
I actually prefer this one with just cucumber. But you can optionally add some finely chopped onion.
Sweet and Sour Asian Dressing:
1 part oil of choice, I use sesame oil (it's milder tasting when it's not toasted)
2 parts apple cider vinegar
1 part raw honey (my preference) or other sweetener (agave)
Sea salt
Pepper to taste
Optional pinch of cayenne pepper

Preparation
1. Try this first using 1 or 2 tablespoons as your 'part'. Scale up from there when you have large quantity of cucumbers to process.
2. What you're after is a slightly sweet yet tangy sauce! It's best to taste test this one as you're preparing it.

Creamy Elote Salad

Necessary products
2 (15-ounce) cans sweet corn, drained
1 (8-ounce) bag chopped romaine lettuce
1 cup halved cherry tomatoes
¼ cup diced red onion
Elote Dressing
¼ cup mayonnaise
¼ cup crumbled Cotija cheese
2 tablespoons sour cream
1 tablespoon paprika
1 tablespoon freshly squeezed lime juice
2 teaspoons ground cayenne pepper
½ teaspoon kosher salt
Preparation

1. In a small bowl, whisk all the ingredients together. Taste for seasoning. Store any leftover dressing in an airtight container in the refrigerator for up to 1 week.
2. In a large bowl, toss all the ingredients with 3 tablespoons of Elote Dressing. Taste and add more dressing, if desired.

Radish, Cucumber, Lox, and Dill Salad

Necessary products
2 large radishes, halved and thinly sliced
4 large Persian cucumbers, halved lengthwise and thinly sliced into half-moons
¼ cup loosely packed fresh dill, minced
1 large garlic clove, minced
6 ounces smoked salmon lox
¼ cup Dill, Lemon, and Garlic Sour Cream Dressing
Preparation

1. Place the radishes, cucumbers, dill, and garlic in a large bowl.
2. Tear the lox into bite-size pieces and add to the bowl. Drizzle with the dressing and toss to combine.
3. Divide the salad between two plates. Serve cold.

Fall Salad

Necessary products

1 pound peeled, cleaned, and diced pumpkin
    (or butternut squash)
½ pound cauliflower, cleaned and diced
3 tablespoons olive oil (divided 1 + 2)
1½ cups cooked cannellini beans (or one
    15-ounce can, drained and rinsed)
2 tart apples, cored and diced
2 tablespoons apple cider vinegar
Salt and pepper to taste
½ cup hazelnuts (preferably toasted),
    roughly chopped

Preparation

1. Mix the pumpkin, cauliflower, a pinch of salt, and one tablespoon of olive oil in an oven pan and bake at 350 degrees for about 30 minutes (stirring a few times for more even cooking) until the pumpkin and cauliflower are tender but not mushy (it's nice if the cauliflower has a bit of crunch left in it). Let the pumpkin and cauliflower cool to room temperature.
2. Combine the pumpkin, cauliflower, beans, and apple in a bowl and mix well.
3. Make the dressing by whisking together the remaining 2 tablespoons of olive oil and the vinegar.
4. Drizzle the dressing over the salad, mix well, taste, and add salt and pepper as desired.
5. Garnish with the chopped hazelnuts.

Raw Carrot & Date Walnut Salad

Necessary products

2 tablespoons apple cider vinegar
¼ cup water
1 teaspoon Dijon mustard
1 tablespoon lemon zest
1 tablespoon pure maple syrup
¼ teaspoon freshly ground black pepper
½ teaspoon cayenne pepper
10 carrots
1 small red onion
4 dates, finely chopped
¼ cup golden raisins
½ cup walnuts, chopped

Preparation

1. In a small bowl, whisk together the vinegar, water, mustard, lemon zest, maple syrup, black pepper, and cayenne pepper to combine. Set aside.
2. Using a mandoline, cut the carrots and red onion with the julienne blade. Transfer to a large bowl and add the dates, raisins, and walnuts. Toss to combine.
3. Pour in the dressing and toss until fully incorporated. Serve immediately or refrigerate in an airtight container overnight.

Carrot Beet Apple Slaw

Prep time: 10 minutes | Cook time: none | Serves 4

Necessary products
1 (15-ounce) can pickled sliced beets, julienned
1 (5-ounce) bag shredded carrots
1 Granny Smith Apple, cored and julienned
Orange-Sesame Dressing
¼ cup vegetable oil
2 tablespoons brown sugar
1 tablespoon rice wine vinegar
1 tablespoon soy sauce
1 tablespoon orange juice
1 tablespoon sesame seeds

Preparation
1. In a small bowl, whisk together all the ingredients until the brown sugar has dissolved. Taste for seasoning. Store any leftover dressing in an airtight container in the refrigerator for up to 1 week.
2. In a large bowl, toss all the ingredients with 2 tablespoons of Orange-Sesame Dressing. Taste and add more dressing, if desired.

Warm Sweet Potato & Brussels Sprout Salad

Prep time: 20 minutes | Cook time: 30 minutes | Serves 4

Necessary products
3 sweet potatoes, peeled and cut into ¼-inch dice
1 teaspoon dried thyme
1 teaspoon garlic powder
½ teaspoon onion powder
1 pound Brussels sprouts
1 cup walnuts, chopped
¼ cup reduced-sugar dried cranberries
2 tablespoons balsamic vinegar
Freshly ground black pepper

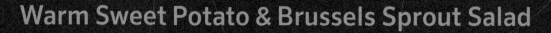

Preparation
1. Preheat the oven to 450°F. Line a baking sheet with parchment paper.
2. Place the sweet potatoes in a colander and rinse. Shake the colander to remove excess water. Sprinkle the damp sweet potatoes with the thyme, garlic powder, and onion powder. Toss to coat evenly with the spices. Transfer to the prepared baking sheet and spread the sweet potatoes in a single layer.
3. Bake for 20 minutes. Flip the sweet potatoes and bake for 10 minutes more, until fork-tender.
4. While the sweet potatoes roast, wash the Brussels sprouts and remove any tough or discolored outer leaves. Using a large chef's knife, halve the Brussels lengthwise. Place them cut-side down and thinly slice the sprouts crosswise into thin shreds. Discard the root end and loosen the shreds.
5. In a large bowl, toss together the Brussels sprouts, sweet potatoes, walnuts, and cranberries. Drizzle with the vinegar and season with pepper.

Chapter 4:

Wholesome Grain, Bean, and Pasta Salads

Calabrian Green Bean Salad

Prep time: 10 minutes | Cook time: 7 minutes | Serves 4

Necessary products
1 pound green beans (tips removed), cut into 1" pieces
20 cherry or grape tomatoes, halved
½ cup black olives, pitted and sliced
2 tablespoons olive oil
3 tablespoons white wine vinegar
2 garlic cloves, peeled and minced
1 tablespoon dried oregano
¼ teaspoon crushed red pepper
Salt and pepper to taste

Preparation
1. Boil the green beans in salted water until tender, about 5-7 minutes depending on thickness. Drain and rinse with cold tap water. Allow them to dry well so that they can absorb the oil and vinegar.
2. Combine the green beans, tomatoes, and olives in a bowl and mix well.
3. Make the dressing by whisking together the olive oil, vinegar, garlic, oregano, and crushed red pepper.
4. Drizzle the dressing over the salad, mix well, taste, and add salt and pepper as desired.

White Bean Tomato Salad

Prep time: 10 minutes | Cook time: 15 minutes | Serves 4

Necessary products
4 cups cooked navy beans, or two 15-ounce cans, drained and rinsed
2 large tomatoes, diced
zest and juice of 2 limes
¼ cup brown rice vinegar
½ cup chopped cilantro
6 green onions (white and green parts), thinly sliced
1 jalapeño pepper, minced (for less heat, remove the seeds)
4 cloves garlic, peeled and minced
1 tablespoon cumin seeds, toasted and ground
salt to taste

Preparation
1. Combine all ingredients in a large bowl and mix well.
2. Chill for 1 hour before serving, if desired.

Black Bean and Orange Salad

Prep time: 20 minutes | Cook time: none | Serves 6

Necessary products
3-4 garlic cloves, minced
1 small red onion, chopped
1 red bell pepper, thinly sliced
1 green bell pepper, thinly sliced
2 tablespoons cilantro
Fresh juice of 4 lemons
1 cup extra-virgin olive oil
1 jalapeño pepper, minced
2 cups cooked black beans
2 oranges, peeled and sectioned
Salt to taste
Black pepper to taste

Preparation
1. Combine first 8 ingredients together in a large bowl.
2. Stir in beans and oranges. Season with salt and pepper. Stir to combine.

Zesty Lemon Orzo Pasta Salad

Prep time: 10 minutes | Cook time: 10 minutes | Serves 4

Necessary products
8 ounces orzo pasta
2 teaspoons kosher salt
1 tablespoon freshly squeezed lemon juice
2 cups arugula
½ cup crumbled feta cheese
¼ cup jarred pickled red cabbage
Lemon-Garlic Vinaigrette
¼ cup extra-virgin olive oil
2 tablespoons freshly squeezed lemon juice
1 tablespoon Dijon mustard
1 teaspoon kosher salt
1 teaspoon red pepper flakes

Preparation
1. In a small bowl, whisk all the ingredients together. Taste for seasoning. Store any leftover dressing in an airtight container in the refrigerator for up to 1 week.
2. Bring a large pot of water to a boil, add the orzo and salt, and cook for 8 to 10 minutes. Drain and place the hot pasta in a large bowl.
3. Add the lemon juice to the orzo and toss. Add the arugula, feta, pickled red cabbage, and 3 tablespoons of Lemon-Garlic Vinaigrette and toss well. Taste and add more dressing, if desired.

Elegant Brunch Snap Peas and Soft-Boiled Egg

Prep time: 10 minutes | Cook time: 12 minutes | Serves 4

Necessary products
4 large eggs
2 to 3 butter lettuce heads, leaves separated
1 cup sugar snap peas
¼ cup thinly sliced red onion
Honey Mustard Dressing
¼ cup mayonnaise
1 tablespoon yellow mustard
1 tablespoon honey
1 teaspoon white vinegar
½ teaspoon kosher salt
Freshly ground black pepper

Preparation
1. In a small bowl, whisk all the ingredients together. Taste for seasoning and add more honey, 1 tablespoon at a time, to your desired sweetness. Store any leftover dressing in an airtight container in the refrigerator for up to 1 week.
2. Bring a saucepan of water to a boil over high heat. Reduce to a simmer, then use a spoon to lower the eggs into the water and cook for 5 minutes for a runny yolk and 7 minutes for a firmer yolk. Remove from the heat and let cool. Carefully peel, cut into halves, and set aside.
3. In a large bowl, gently toss the lettuce, snap peas, and red onion together with 2 tablespoons of Honey Mustard dressing. Taste and add more dressing, if desired. Serve with 2 egg halves on each plate.

Mixed Bean and Pumpkin Salad

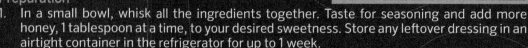
Prep time: 10 minutes | Cook time: 30 minutes | Serves 4

Necessary products
1 pound peeled, cleaned, and diced pumpkin
    (or butternut squash)
½ yellow or white onion, peeled and diced
Leaves from 2 sprigs of rosemary, roughly
    chopped
1 tablespoon thyme leaves
3 tablespoons olive oil (divided 1 + 2)
1½ cups cooked cannellini beans (or one
    15-ounce can, drained and rinsed)
1½ cups cooked borlotti (or pinto) beans (or
    one 15-ounce can, drained and rinsed)
3 ounces baby spinach
Juice of 1 lemon
Salt and pepper to taste

Preparation
1. Mix the pumpkin, onion, rosemary, thyme, and one tablespoon of olive oil in an oven pan and bake at 350 degrees for about 30 minutes (stirring a few times for even cooking) until the pumpkin is tender but not mushy.
2. Let the pumpkin cool to room temperature.
3. Combine the pumpkin, beans, and spinach in a bowl and mix well.
4. Make the dressing by whisking together the remaining 2 tablespoons of olive oil and the lemon juice.
5. Drizzle the dressing over the salad, mix well, taste, and add salt and pepper as desired.

Balela Salad

Necessary products
1 (15-ounce) can chickpeas
1 (15-ounce) can black beans
1 (15-ounce) can kidney beans
1 medium red onion, finely chopped
1 large jalapeño pepper, minced
2 garlic cloves, minced
Ground cumin, for seasoning
Salt
Freshly ground black pepper
½ cup Herb Vinaigrette

Preparation
1. Drain and rinse the chickpeas, black beans, and kidney beans. Place them in a large glass bowl.
2. Stir the red onion, jalapeño, and garlic into the beans. Season the salad with cumin, salt, and pepper. Add the vinaigrette and toss to combine.
3. For the ideal flavor, refrigerate the salad for at least 30 minutes before dividing among four plates and serving.

Italian Bean and Rice Salad

Necessary products
2 cups cooked long-grain rice
1 cup cooked beans
1 cup cherry tomatoes, halved
2 ounces Cheddar cheese, shredded
1/4 cup Italian dressing
1 tablespoon balsamic vinegar
1 tablespoon lemon zest
Sea salt to taste
Black pepper to taste
Lettuce leaves for garnish

Preparation
1. Combine rice, beans, tomatoes, and cheese in a large bowl. Toss to combine.
2. Pour Italian dressing and vinegar over the mixture in the bowl.
3. Toss again and sprinkle lemon zest. Season with salt and pepper to taste and adjust the seasonings. Serve on lettuce leaves.

Rice Noodle Salad with Orange and Edamame

Prep time: 30 minutes | Cook time: 5 minutes | Serves 2

Necessary products
For the Salad:
8 oz rice noodles
1 cup shelled edamame, cooked
1 orange, peeled and segmented
1 red bell pepper, thinly sliced
1 carrot, julienned
2 green onions, sliced
1/4 cup fresh cilantro, chopped
1/4 cup fresh mint leaves, chopped
Sesame seeds for garnish (optional)
For the Dressing:
3 tablespoons soy sauce
2 tablespoons rice vinegar
2 tablespoons sesame oil
1 tablespoon honey or maple syrup
1 clove garlic, minced
1 teaspoon fresh ginger, grated
Zest and juice of 1 lime

Preparation
1. Cook the rice noodles according to package instructions. Once cooked, drain and rinse them under cold water to stop the cooking process. Set aside.
2. In a large mixing bowl, combine the cooked rice noodles, edamame, orange segments, sliced red bell pepper, julienned carrot, green onions, cilantro, and mint.
3. In a small bowl, whisk together the soy sauce, rice vinegar, sesame oil, honey or maple syrup, minced garlic, grated ginger, lime zest, and lime juice to make the dressing.
4. Pour the dressing over the salad and toss everything together until well combined. Make sure the noodles and vegetables are evenly coated with the dressing.
5. Allow the salad to sit for a few minutes to let the flavors meld together. You can also refrigerate it for a couple of hours to serve it chilled.
6. Before serving, garnish the salad with sesame seeds if desired.

Snap Pea Broccoli Slaw

Prep time: 10 minutes | Cook time: none | Serves 4

Necessary products
2 cups premade broccoli slaw mix
2 cups chopped snap peas, sliced diagonally
¼ cup thinly sliced red onion
Orange-Sesame Dressing
¼ cup vegetable oil
2 tablespoons brown sugar
1 tablespoon rice wine vinegar
1 tablespoon soy sauce
1 tablespoon orange juice
1 tablespoon sesame seeds

Preparation
1. In a small bowl, whisk together all the ingredients until the brown sugar has dissolved. Store any leftover dressing in an airtight container in the refrigerator for up to 1 week.
2. In a large bowl, toss all the ingredients with 2 tablespoons of Orange-Sesame Dressing. Taste and add more dressing, if desired.

Charred Poblano, Corn, and Wild Rice Salad

Prep time: 30 minutes | Cook time: 5 minutes | Serves 4

Necessary products
For the Salad:
1 cup wild rice, cooked according
    to package instructions
2 poblano peppers
2 cups fresh or frozen corn kernels
1 red onion, finely chopped
1/2 cup fresh cilantro, chopped
1 avocado, diced
1 lime, juiced
Salt and pepper to taste
For the Dressing:
3 tablespoons olive oil
2 tablespoons red wine vinegar
1 teaspoon honey or maple syrup
1 teaspoon ground cumin
Salt and pepper to taste

Preparation
1. Cook the wild rice according to package instructions. Once cooked, allow it to cool to room temperature.
2. Char the poblano peppers over an open flame on a gas stove or under the broiler until the skin is blistered and blackened. Place the charred poblanos in a bowl, cover with plastic wrap, and let them steam for about 10 minutes. After steaming, peel off the charred skin, remove the seeds, and dice the peppers.
3. In a large mixing bowl, combine the cooked wild rice, diced poblano peppers, corn kernels, chopped red onion, cilantro, and diced avocado.
4. In a small bowl, whisk together the olive oil, red wine vinegar, honey or maple syrup, ground cumin, salt, and pepper to make the dressing.
5. Pour the dressing over the salad and toss everything together until well combined.
6. Squeeze the juice of one lime over the salad and toss again.Adjust the seasoning with salt and pepper to taste. Chill the salad in the refrigerator for at least 30 minutes before serving to allow the flavors to meld.
7. Serve the Charred Poblano, Corn, and Wild Rice Salad as a refreshing and flavorful side dish.

Chapter 5:

Tasty Tofu and Egg Salads

Spinach Salad with Poached Eggs and Bacon

Prep time: 30 minutes | Cook time: none | Serves 6

Necessary products
1 lb. bacon, chopped
1 tablespoon Dijon mustard
1 tablespoon balsamic vinegar
1 tablespoon lemon juice
1 tablespoon honey
1 teaspoon sea salt
1/4 teaspoon freshly ground black pepper
1 Pound Fresh baby spinach; washed and patted dry
1 cup scallions, finely chopped
2 cloves garlic, minced
4 poached eggs

Preparation
1. In a wide skillet, over medium heat, brown the bacon until it is crisp, for 6 to 8 minutes. Set aside, reserving the bacon fat.
2. To make the vinaigrette: Whisk together the reserved bacon fat, mustard, vinegar, lemon and honey. Whisk until the ingredients are well combined.
3. Season with salt and black pepper.
4. In a large bowl, combine baby spinach with scallions and garlic. Drizzle the vinaigrette and toss to combine. Taste and adjust the seasonings.
5. Arrange spinach mixture on the serving plates. Place bacon and eggs on top and serve immediately.

Avocado and Bacon Egg Salad

Prep time: 15 minutes | Cook time: 15 minutes| Serves 4

Necessary products
6 Hard-boiled eggs, chopped
2 Avocados, mashed
6 slices Cooked bacon, crumbled
1/4 cup Red onion, finely diced
1 tablespoon Dijon mustard
Salt and pepper to taste
Chopped parsley for garnish

Preparation
1. In a bowl, combine chopped hard-boiled eggs with mashed avocado.
2. Add crumbled cooked bacon, finely diced red onion, and Dijon mustard.
3. Season with salt and pepper to taste.
4. Garnish with chopped parsley and serve as a sandwich or on lettuce leaves.

Asian Sesame Tofu Salad

Prep time: 15 minutes | Cook time: 10 minutes| Serves 4

Necessary products
1 block (about 14 oz) Firm tofu, cubed
8 cups Mixed salad greens
2 Carrots, julienned
1 Red bell pepper, thinly sliced
1 cup Edamame beans, steamed
4 Green onions, chopped
2 tablespoons Sesame seeds

Dressing:
1/4 cup Soy sauce
2 tablespoons Sesame oil
2 tablespoons Rice vinegar
2 tablespoons Honey
1 tablespoon Ginger, grated

Preparation
1. Pan-fry tofu cubes until golden brown.
2. In a large bowl, combine salad greens, julienned carrots, sliced red bell pepper, steamed edamame, and chopped green onions.
3. Whisk together soy sauce, sesame oil, rice vinegar, honey, and grated ginger for the dressing.
4. Toss the tofu with the salad, drizzle with the dressing, and sprinkle sesame seeds on top.

Greek Tofu Salad

Prep time: 15 minutes | Cook time: 15 minutes| Serves 4

Necessary products
1 block (about 14 oz) Extra-firm tofu, diced
1 Cucumber, diced
1 cup Cherry tomatoes, halved
1/2 cup Kalamata olives, sliced
1/2 Red onion, thinly sliced
1/2 cup Feta cheese, crumbled
1 tablespoon Fresh oregano, chopped

Dressing:
1/4 cup Olive oil
2 tablespoons Lemon juice
Salt and pepper to taste

Preparation
1. Bake or pan-fry the diced extra-firm tofu until crispy.
2. In a large bowl, combine diced cucumber, halved cherry tomatoes, sliced Kalamata olives, thinly sliced red onion, and crumbled feta cheese.
3. In a separate bowl, whisk together 1/4 cup olive oil, 2 tablespoons lemon juice, salt, and pepper to create the dressing.
4. Toss the crispy tofu with the salad and drizzle the dressing over the top. Sprinkle with fresh oregano.

Curry Egg Salad

Prep time: 15 minutes | Cook time: 15 minutes| Serves 4

Necessary products
6 hard-boiled eggs, chopped
1/2 cup greek yogurt
1 tablespoon curry powder
2 tablespoons mango chutney
1/2 cup celery, finely chopped
4 green onions, sliced
Salt and pepper to taste
Raisins (optional)

Preparation
1. In a bowl, mix 6 chopped hard-boiled eggs with 1/2 cup Greek yogurt, 1 tablespoon curry powder, and 2 tablespoons mango chutney.
2. Add 1/2 cup finely chopped celery, sliced 4 green onions, and optional raisins.
3. Season with salt and pepper to taste.
4. Serve on bread or with crackers.

Tofu and Avocado Salad

Prep time: 15 minutes | Cook time: 10 minutes| Serves 4

Necessary products
1 block (about 14 oz) Extra-firm tofu, cubed
8 cups Mixed salad greens
2 Avocados, sliced
1 cup Radishes, thinly sliced
1 cup Cherry tomatoes, halved
1/4 cup Pumpkin seeds
1/4 cup Cilantro, chopped
Dressing:
3 tablespoons Lime juice
2 tablespoons Olive oil
1 teaspoon Cumin
1 teaspoon Garlic powder
Salt and pepper to taste

Preparation
1. Sauté the cubed extra-firm tofu until golden brown.
2. In a large salad bowl, combine 8 cups of mixed greens, sliced avocados, thinly sliced radishes, halved cherry tomatoes, pumpkin seeds, and chopped cilantro.
3. In a separate bowl, whisk together 3 tablespoons lime juice, 2 tablespoons olive oil, 1 teaspoon cumin, 1 teaspoon garlic powder, salt, and pepper to create the dressing.
4. Toss the sautéed tofu with the salad and drizzle the dressing over the top.
5. Enjoy your Tofu and Avocado Salad!

Mango and Tofu Summer Salad

Prep time: 15 minutes | Cook time: 10 minutes| Serves 4

Necessary products
1 block (about 14 oz) Firm tofu, sliced
1 head Romaine lettuce, chopped
2 Mangoes, diced
1 Red bell pepper, chopped
1/2 Red onion, thinly sliced
1/4 cup Mint leaves, chopped
1/4 cup Cashews, chopped
Dressing:
3 tablespoons Lime juice
2 tablespoons Olive oil
2 tablespoons Agave nectar or honey
1/2 teaspoon Chili flakes (optional)
Salt and pepper to taste

Preparation
1. Grill or pan-fry the sliced firm tofu until grill marks appear.
2. In a large bowl, combine chopped Romaine lettuce, diced mango, chopped red bell pepper, thinly sliced red onion, chopped mint leaves, and chopped cashews.
3. In a separate bowl, whisk together 3 tablespoons lime juice, 2 tablespoons olive oil, 2 tablespoons agave nectar or honey, 1/2 teaspoon chili flakes (optional), salt, and pepper to create the dressing.
4. Arrange the grilled tofu on top of the salad and drizzle the dressing over the salad.
5. Enjoy your Mango and Tofu Summer Salad!

Classic Egg Salad

Prep time: 15 minutes | Cook time: 10 minutes| Serves 4

Necessary products
6 Hard-boiled eggs, chopped
1/2 cup Mayonnaise
1 tablespoon Dijon mustard
Salt and pepper to taste
1/4 cup chopped celery (optional)
2 tablespoons chopped green onions (optional)

Preparation
1. In a bowl, combine 6 chopped hard-boiled eggs with 1/2 cup mayonnaise and 1 tablespoon Dijon mustard.
2. Season with salt and pepper to taste.
3. Add 1/4 cup chopped celery and 2 tablespoons chopped green onions if desired.
4. Mix well and serve on bread or with crackers.

Spinach Egg Salad with Dijon Vinaigrette

Prep time: 10 minutes | Cook time: none | Serves 1

Necessary products
4 tablespoons extra-virgin olive oil
1 tablespoon white wine vinegar
1 tablespoon lemon juice
1/2 teaspoon Dijon mustard
Sea salt to taste
Black pepper to taste
2 cups spinach leaves, washed and
    torn into bite-sized pieces
1/2 cup grape tomatoes, sliced
1 hard-boiled egg, chopped
2 rashers bacon, cooked and sliced
1 pita bread, cut into quarters

Preparation
1. To make the salad dressing: In a medium bowl, whisk the ingredients for dressing. Whisk until all ingredients are well combined.
2. Arrange spinach leaves in a serving bowl. Place tomatoes, eggs, and bacon. Drizzle the dressing.
3. Serve with the hot pita bread.

Creamy Avocado Egg Salad

Prep time: 15 minutes | Cook time: 20 minutes| Serves 4

Necessary products
6 hard-boiled eggs, peeled and chopped
1 ripe avocado, peeled and mashed
2 tablespoons Greek yogurt or mayonnaise
1 tablespoon lime juice
1 tablespoon finely chopped red onion
1 tablespoon chopped fresh cilantro or parsley
Salt and pepper to taste
Bread or lettuce leaves, for serving (optional)

Preparation
1. In a mixing bowl, combine the chopped eggs, mashed avocado, Greek yogurt or mayonnaise, lime juice, chopped red onion, and chopped cilantro or parsley. Stir until well combined and creamy.
2. Season the egg salad with salt and pepper to taste. Adjust the seasoning as needed.
3. Serve the creamy avocado egg salad on bread to make sandwiches, or spoon it onto lettuce leaves for a lighter option.
4. Enjoy your delicious and nutritious avocado egg salad!

Caprese Egg Salad

Prep time: 15 minutes | Cook time: 20 minutes| Serves 4

Necessary products
6 hard-boiled eggs, sliced
1 cup cherry tomatoes, halved
8 oz fresh mozzarella, diced
1/2 cup fresh basil leaves, torn
balsamic glaze, for drizzling
2 tablespoons olive oil
Salt and pepper to taste

Preparation
1. Arrange 6 sliced hard-boiled eggs, 1 cup halved cherry tomatoes, 8 oz diced fresh mozzarella, and 1/2 cup torn fresh basil leaves on a plate.
2. Drizzle with balsamic glaze and 2 tablespoons olive oil.
3. Season with salt and pepper to taste.
4. Serve as a refreshing and flavorful Caprese-inspired egg salad.

Warm Bell Pepper and Tofu Salad

Prep time: 5 minutes | Cook time: 15 minutes |Serves 4

Necessary products
1 (14-ounce) tofu block, pressed and cubed
4 bell peppers, deveined and halved
2 scallions, chopped
2 tablespoons fresh lemon juice
2 tablespoons extra-virgin olive oil

Preparation
1. Heat up a lightly greased cast-iron skillet over medium-high heat. Then, cook the tofu cubes approximately 3 minutes, gently stirring to ensure even cooking; reserve.
2. Brush the same skillet with cooking oil and fry the peppers until just tender and charred or about 5 minutes. Transfer them to a salad bowl.
3. Toss with the scallions, lemon juice, and olive oil. Afterwards, top your salad with the fried tofu and serve immediately.

Bon appétit!

Chapter 6:

Fresh Fish and Seafood Salads

Pineapple Coconut Shrimp Salad

Prep time: 10 minutes | Cook time: none | Serves 4

Necessary products
1 (8 to 10-ounce) box coconut shrimp
1 (8-ounce) bag mixed greens
1 cup pineapple salsa
¼ cup diced English cucumber
½ cup halved cherry tomatoes
Honey-Lime Vinaigrette
¼ cup extra-virgin olive oil
2 tablespoons freshly squeezed lime juice
2 tablespoons honey
1 teaspoon kosher salt
½ teaspoon red pepper flakes

Preparation
1. In a small bowl, whisk all the ingredients together. Taste for seasoning. Store any leftover dressing in an airtight container in the refrigerator for up to 1 week.
2. Heat the coconut shrimp according to package instructions.
3. In a large bowl, toss the mixed greens, pineapple salsa, cucumber, and cherry tomatoes together with 3 tablespoons of Honey-Lime Vinaigrette. Taste and add more dressing, if desired.
4. Top with the coconut shrimp to serve.

Creamy Tuna and Cabbage Salad

Prep time: 20 minutes | Cook time: none | Serves 4

Necessary products
1 can tuna fish
1 cup cabbage, shredded
1 cup celery, thinly sliced
1 medium onion, chopped
4 tablespoons mayonnaise
Cream salad dressing to taste
1 handful fresh parsley, roughly chopped

Preparation
1. Drain the oil from the tuna fish. Remove the bones from the fish.
2. Add cabbage, celery, onion, mayonnaise and dressing. Stir well to combine. Transfer the salad to a serving bowl.
3. Taste and adjust the seasonings. Sprinkle the parsley and serve at room temperature or chilled.

Shaved Brussels Sprout and Shrimp Salad

Prep time: 10 minutes | Cook time: 5 minutes | Serves 4

Necessary products
For the Salad:
1 lb large shrimp, peeled and deveined
1 lb Brussels sprouts, trimmed and thinly sliced
1/2 cup cherry tomatoes, halved
1/4 cup red onion, thinly sliced
1/4 cup feta cheese, crumbled (optional)
1/4 cup almonds, sliced and toasted
For the Dressing:
3 tablespoons olive oil
2 tablespoons lemon juice
1 tablespoon Dijon mustard
1 clove garlic, minced
Salt and pepper to taste

Preparation
1. In a large skillet, cook the shrimp over medium-high heat until they are pink and opaque, about 2-3 minutes per side. Remove from heat and let them cool.
2. In a large mixing bowl, combine the shaved Brussels sprouts, cherry tomatoes, red onion, and, if desired, crumbled feta cheese.
3. In a separate small bowl, whisk together the olive oil, lemon juice, Dijon mustard, minced garlic, salt, and pepper to make the dressing.
4. Add the cooked shrimp to the Brussels sprout mixture.
5. Pour the dressing over the salad and toss everything together until well combined.
6. Top the salad with toasted sliced almonds for added crunch.
7. Adjust the seasoning with salt and pepper to taste.
8. Chill the salad in the refrigerator for about 30 minutes before serving to allow the flavors to meld.
9. Serve the Shaved Brussels Sprout and Shrimp Salad as a light and refreshing meal.

Tuna Salad with Lime Mayo

Prep time: 5 minutes | Cook time: 5 minutes | Serves 2

Necessary products
1 cup canned tuna, drained
1 tsp onion flakes
3 tbsp mayonnaise
1 cup romaine lettuce, shredded
1 tbsp lime juice
Sea salt to taste
6 black olives, pitted and sliced

Preparation
1. Combine tuna, mayonnaise, lime juice, and salt to taste in a bowl and mix. In a salad platter, arrange lettuce and onion flakes.
2. Spread the tuna mixture over; top with black olives, and serve well-chilled.

French Salmon Salad

Necessary products
2 cups salmon, boneless and skinless
1 cup celery, diced
1 medium onion, chopped
4 sweet pickles, finely chopped
French dressing
Salad dressing of choice
Iceberg Salad leaves for garnish

Preparation
1. Slice the salmon into medium-sized chunks. Add the celery, onion, and pickles. Stir to combine.
2. Marinate this mixture with the French dressing.
3. Drain and serve with your favorite salad dressing, garnished with Iceberg Salad.

Tuna Salad Wraps

Necessary products
2 cups canned tuna fish, drained
1 cup green onions, thinly sliced
2 cloves garlic, minced
1 tablespoon yellow mustard
6 large lettuce leaves
2 large carrots, shredded
2 large cucumbers, thinly sliced
Salt to taste
Black pepper to taste
Red pepper flakes to taste
Parsley for garnish, chopped

Preparation
1. In a medium bowl, combine tuna with onions, garlic and mustard. Stir to combine ingredients.
2. To make the wraps: Place tuna spread in a center of lettuce leaf. Then place carrots and cucumbers on top. Season with salt, pepper, and red pepper flakes.
3. Make wraps, sprinkle with chopped parsley and serve chilled.

Tuna Niçoise Salad

Prep time: 15 minutes | Cook time: 5 minutes | Serves 3 or 4

Necessary products

For the Salad:
1 lb small red potatoes, halved
8 oz green beans, trimmed
4 large eggs
1 cup cherry tomatoes, halved
1/2 cup Niçoise olives
4 cups mixed salad greens (such as arugula or mesclun)
2 (5 oz) cans of tuna, drained

For the Dressing:
1/4 cup red wine vinegar
1/2 cup extra-virgin olive oil
1 tablespoon Dijon mustard
1 clove garlic, minced
Salt and pepper to taste

Preparation

1. In a large pot of salted boiling water, cook the halved red potatoes until they are fork-tender, about 15 minutes. During the last 5 minutes of cooking, add the green beans to the boiling water. Drain the potatoes and green beans, then run them under cold water to stop the cooking process.
2. In a separate pot, place the eggs and cover them with cold water. Bring the water to a boil, then reduce the heat and simmer for 9-10 minutes. Transfer the eggs to a bowl of ice water to cool. Once cooled, peel the eggs and cut them in half.
3. In a large serving platter or individual plates, arrange the salad greens. Top with the cooked potatoes, green beans, halved cherry tomatoes, Niçoise olives, and tuna.
4. Arrange the boiled egg halves on top of the salad.
5. In a small bowl, whisk together the red wine vinegar, olive oil, Dijon mustard, minced garlic, salt, and pepper to make the dressing. Drizzle the dressing over the Tuna Niçoise Salad.
6. Serve immediately and enjoy this classic French salad!

Seafood Quinoa Salad with Lemon-Dill Vinaigrette

Prep time: 20 minutes | Cook time: 15 minutes | Serves 4

Necessary products
1 cup quinoa
1 pound shrimp, peeled and deveined
1 pound sea scallops
Salt and pepper
2 tablespoons olive oil
1 cup cherry tomatoes, halved
1 cucumber, diced
1/2 cup red onion, finely chopped
1/4 cup fresh parsley, chopped
Lemon-Dill Vinaigrette:
1/4 cup olive oil
2 tablespoons fresh lemon juice
1 tablespoon Dijon mustard
1 tablespoon honey
2 tablespoons fresh dill, chopped
Salt and pepper to taste

Preparation
1. Cook quinoa according to package instructions. Fluff with a fork and set aside.
2. Season shrimp and scallops with salt and pepper. In a skillet, heat olive oil over medium-high heat. Cook shrimp and scallops until they are opaque and cooked through. Remove from heat.
3. In a large bowl, combine cooked quinoa, shrimp, scallops, cherry tomatoes, cucumber, red onion, and fresh parsley.
4. In a separate small bowl, whisk together the ingredients for the Lemon-Dill Vinaigrette until well combined.
5. Drizzle the vinaigrette over the seafood and quinoa mixture. Toss gently to coat evenly.
6. Serve the seafood quinoa salad at room temperature or chilled. Enjoy this refreshing and protein-packed seafood salad!

Crab Salad with Baby Asparagus

Prep time: 15 minutes | Cook time: none | Serves 4

Necessary products
1 cup mayonnaise
2 teaspoon Creole mustard
1 tablespoon balsamic vinegar
1 tablespoon lemon juice
2 cloves garlic, chopped
1 tablespoon tarragon leaves, finely chopped
1/4 cup green onion, finely chopped
1 lb. lump crab meat
1 teaspoon sea salt
1/4 teaspoon freshly ground black pepper
1/2 teaspoon sweet paprika
1/2 lb. baby asparagus
2 tablespoons olive oil
12 zucchini flowers
Lemon wedges for garnish

Preparation
1. To make the dressing: In a medium bowl, whisk the mayonnaise, mustard, vinegar, lemon juice, garlic, tarragon and green onions.
2. Fold in the crab meat. Season with salt, black pepper and paprika. Reserve.
3. In another bowl, combine the asparagus and olive oil.
4. Divide the asparagus mixture among serving plates and spoon the crab salad with dressing. Place zucchini flowers on the crab salad. Garnish with lemon wedges.

Shrimp and Cauliflower Salad with Dill Dressing

Prep time: 1 hour 10 minutes | Cook time: 20 minutes | Serves 4

Necessary products
5 cups cauliflower florets
1/3 cup celery, diced
2 cups large shrimp, cooked
1 tbsp bill, chopped
½ cup mayonnaise
1 tsp apple cider vinegar
¼ tsp celery seeds
2 tbsp lemon juice
2 tsp swerve sweetener
Salt and black pepper to taste

Preparation
1. Combine cauliflower, celery, shrimp, and dill in a large bowl. Whisk mayonnaise, vinegar, celery seeds, sweetener, and lemon juice in another bowl.
2. Season with salt. Pour the dressing over the salad, and gently toss to combine. Serve cold.

Creamy Oysters Salad

Prep time: 25 minutes | Cook time: none | Serves 8

Necessary products
1 bottle oysters
1 lettuce
Juice of 1 fresh lemon
3 tablespoons mayonnaise
3 tablespoons salad dressing

Preparation
1. Strain away the liquid from a bottle of oysters. Pour this liquid into a large saucepan. Bring to a boil and add the oysters. Cook for 5 to 6 minutes or until the liquid is mostly evaporated.
2. Place the lettuce on the bottom of a bowl. Then place the oysters mixture (without any liquid) and add lemon juice, mayonnaise and salad dressing.

Beachy Cold Shrimp Corn Salad

Prep time: 10 minutes | Cook time: none | Serves 4

Necessary products
3 cups chopped frozen precooked shrimp, thawed
2 (15-ounce) cans corn, drained and rinsed
½ cup chopped scallions, green part only
¼ cup chopped fresh cilantro
1 jalapeño pepper, seeded and finely diced
1 teaspoon kosher salt
Chili-Lime Vinaigrette
2 tablespoons extra-virgin olive oil
2 tablespoons freshly squeezed lime juice
1 teaspoon ground cayenne pepper
½ teaspoon kosher salt
½ teaspoon ground cumin

Preparation
1. In a small bowl, whisk all the ingredients together. Taste for seasoning.
2. In a large bowl, toss all the ingredients together with all of the Chili-Lime Vinaigrette. Marinate for 10 minutes, then serve.

Cajun Shrimp Salad

Necessary products

1 pound large shrimp, peeled and deveined
2 tablespoons avocado oil
2 cloves garlic, minced
2 teaspoons dried basil
1 teaspoon dried thyme leaves
1¾ teaspoons paprika
¾ teaspoon ground black pepper
½ teaspoon finely ground sea salt
⅛ teaspoon cayenne pepper
1 bunch asparagus, woody ends snapped
    off, cut in half crosswise
Salad:
1 large head butter lettuce, chopped
1 medium Hass avocado, peeled, pitted, and
    sliced (about 4 oz of flesh)
1 small red onion, thinly sliced
½ cup creamy Italian dressing or other
    creamy salad dressing of choice

Preparation

1. Place the shrimp, oil, garlic, basil, thyme, paprika, black pepper, salt, and cayenne in a large frying pan. Toss to coat the shrimp, then turn the heat to medium and cook until the shrimp is pink, about 5 minutes.
2. Add the asparagus, cover, and cook for 10 minutes, or until the asparagus is fork-tender.
3. Meanwhile, divide the lettuce, avocado, and onion evenly among 4 salad plates. When the shrimp and asparagus are done, divide the mixture evenly among the plates, drizzle each salad with 2 tablespoons of dressing, and enjoy!

Salmon Salad Cups

Necessary products

12 ounces canned salmon (no salt added)
3 tablespoons prepared horseradish
1 tablespoon chopped fresh dill
2 teaspoons lemon juice
½ teaspoon finely ground sea salt
½ teaspoon ground black pepper
12 butter lettuce leaves (from 1 head)
½ cup mayonnaise

Preparation

1. Place the salmon, horseradish, dill, lemon juice, salt, and pepper in a medium-sized bowl. Stir until the ingredients are fully incorporated.
2. Set the lettuce leaves on a serving plate. Fill each leaf with 2 tablespoons of the salmon salad mixture and top with 2 teaspoons of mayonnaise.

Chapter 7:

Scrumptious Chicken Salads

Cajun Lime Avocado Chicken Salad

Necessary products
1 (8-ounce) bag chopped romaine lettuce
3 cups sliced rotisserie chicken
2 teaspoons Cajun seasoning
1 tablespoon freshly squeezed lime juice
1 avocado, sliced
1 (15-ounce) can corn, drained and rinsed
¼ cup thinly sliced red onion
Cajun Dressing
¼ cup mayonnaise
2 tablespoons plain whole milk Greek yogurt
1 tablespoon freshly squeezed lemon juice
1½ teaspoons Cajun seasoning
1 teaspoon paprika
1 teaspoon kosher salt

Preparation
1. In a small bowl, whisk all the ingredients together. Taste for seasoning. Store any leftover dressing in an airtight container in the refrigerator for up to 1 week.
2. Arrange the lettuce on a large platter and set aside.
3. In a large bowl, toss the chicken, Cajun seasoning, and lime juice together until the chicken is coated.
4. Place the chicken on top of the romaine lettuce, then add the avocado, corn, and red onion.
5. Drizzle the salad with 3 tablespoons of Cajun Dressing. Taste and add more dressing, if desired.

Old-Fashioned Chicken Salad

Necessary products
Poached Chicken:
2 chicken breasts, skinless and boneless
1/2 teaspoon salt
2 bay laurels
1/2 teaspoon salt
2 bay laurels
1 thyme sprig
1 rosemary sprig
4 scallions, trimmed and thinly sliced
1 tablespoon fresh coriander, chopped
1 teaspoon Dijon mustard
2 teaspoons freshly squeezed lemon juice
1 cup mayonnaise, preferably homemade

Preparation
1. Place all ingredients for the poached chicken in a stockpot; cover with water and bring to a rolling boil.
2. Turn the heat to medium-low and let it simmer for about 15 minutes or until a meat thermometer reads 165 degrees F. Let the poached chicken cool to room temperature.
3. Cut into strips and transfer to a nice salad bowl.
4. Toss the poached chicken with the salad ingredients; serve well chilled and enjoy!

Chicken Gyro Salad

Necessary products

1 pound chicken breast
Salt
Freshly ground black pepper
1 tablespoon shawarma seasoning
2 tablespoons extra-virgin olive oil
7 or 8 cups shredded romaine lettuce
2 Persian cucumbers, sliced
2 cups cherry tomatoes, halved
1 cup crumbled feta cheese
6 tablespoons Dill, Lemon, and Garlic
    Sour Cream Dressing

Preparation

1. Use salt, pepper, and the shawarma seasoning to season the chicken and the olive oil to cook it.
2. Place the romaine lettuce, cucumbers, tomatoes, and feta in a large bowl and toss to combine.
3. Slice the chicken into bite-size strips.
4. Divide the salad among four bowls. Layer the chicken strips over the salad and drizzle it all with the dressing. Serve while the chicken is warm.

Mom's Chicken Salad

Necessary products

2 chicken thighs, skinless
Sea salt and cayenne pepper, to season
1/2 teaspoon Dijon mustard
1 tablespoon red wine vinegar
1/4 cup mayonnaise
1 small-sized celery stalk, chopped
2 spring onion stalks, chopped
1/2 head Romaine lettuce, torn into pieces
1/2 cucumber, sliced

Preparation

1. Fry the chicken thighs until thoroughly heated and crunchy on the outside; an instant-read thermometer should read about 165 degrees F.
2. Discard the bones and chop the meat.
3. Place the other ingredients in a serving bowl and stir until everything is well incorporated. Layer the chopped chicken thighs over the salad.
4. Serve well chilled and enjoy!

Pear, Pecan, and Chicken Salad

Prep time: 20 minutes | Cook time: 5 minutes | Serves 3

Necessary products
1 cup quinoa
½ pound chicken breast
Salt
Freshly ground black pepper
2 tablespoons pecan oil
2 ripe pears, thinly sliced
½ cup toasted pecans
1 cup mixed greens
6 tablespoons Honey-Mustard Vinaigrette

Preparation
1. Cook quinoa following the package instructions. Fluff with a fork.
2. Season and cook chicken in pecan oil. Slice into bite-size pieces.
3. In three bowls, arrange quinoa, chicken, pear slices, toasted pecans, and mixed greens. Drizzle with Honey-Mustard Vinaigrette. Serve and relish the delicious combination.

Apple, Walnut, and Chicken Salad

Prep time: 20 minutes | Cook time: 5 minutes | Serves 3

Necessary products
1 cup quinoa
½ pound chicken breast
Salt
Freshly ground black pepper
2 tablespoons walnut oil
1 medium apple, thinly sliced
½ cup chopped walnuts
1 cup arugula
6 tablespoons Apple-Dijon Dressing

Preparation
1. Cook the quinoa as directed. Fluff with a fork.
2. Season and cook the chicken in walnut oil. Slice into bite-size pieces.
3. In three bowls, arrange quinoa, chicken, apple slices, walnuts, and arugula. Drizzle with Apple-Dijon Dressing. Serve and savor.

Roasted Vegetable and Chicken Salad

Prep time: 25 minutes | Cook time: 20 minutes | Serves 4

Necessary products
1 cup quinoa
½ pound chicken breast
Salt
Freshly ground black pepper
2 tablespoons olive oil
1 cup cherry tomatoes, halved
1 zucchini, sliced
1 red bell pepper, sliced
1 cup broccoli florets
6 tablespoons Balsamic-Dijon Vinaigrette

Preparation
1. Cook quinoa following package instructions. Fluff with a fork.
2. Season chicken with salt and pepper. Roast in the oven or grill until fully cooked. Slice into bite-size pieces.
3. In a pan, heat olive oil and sauté cherry tomatoes, zucchini, red bell pepper, and broccoli until tender.
4. Divide quinoa, roasted chicken, and the sautéed vegetables among four bowls. Drizzle with Balsamic-Dijon Vinaigrette. Serve and enjoy this hearty and flavorful roasted vegetable and chicken salad.

Grilled Chicken Salad

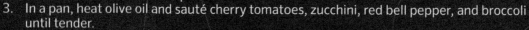

Prep time: 5 minutes | Cook time:20 minutes |Serves 2

Necessary products
2 chicken breasts
2 tablespoons extra-virgin olive oil
4 tablespoons apple cider vinegar
1 cup grape tomatoes, halved
1 Lebanese cucumber, thinly sliced

Preparation
1. Preheat your grill to medium-high temperature. Now, grill the chicken breasts for 5 to 7 minutes on each side.
2. Slice the chicken into strips and transfer them to a nice salad bowl. Toss with the olive oil, vinegar, grape tomatoes, and cucumber.
3. Garnish with fresh snipped chives if desired. Bon appétit!

Thai Chicken and Peanut Salad

Prep time: 30 minutes | Cook time: 5 minutes | Serves 4

Necessary products

For the Salad:
1 lb boneless, skinless chicken breasts, grilled or cooked and shredded
8 oz rice noodles, cooked according to package instructions
1 red bell pepper, thinly sliced
1 cucumber, julienned
1 carrot, julienned
1 cup shredded cabbage
1/2 cup fresh cilantro, chopped
1/4 cup fresh mint leaves, chopped
1/4 cup peanuts, chopped
Lime wedges for serving

For the Peanut Dressing:
1/3 cup creamy peanut butter
3 tablespoons soy sauce
2 tablespoons rice vinegar
2 tablespoons honey or maple syrup
1 tablespoon sesame oil
1 clove garlic, minced
1 teaspoon fresh ginger, grated
2 tablespoons water (adjust for desired consistency)

Preparation

1. In a large bowl, combine the shredded chicken, cooked rice noodles, sliced red bell pepper, julienned cucumber, julienned carrot, shredded cabbage, chopped cilantro, and chopped mint.
2. In a small bowl, whisk together the peanut butter, soy sauce, rice vinegar, honey or maple syrup, sesame oil, minced garlic, and grated ginger to make the peanut dressing. Add water gradually to achieve the desired consistency.
3. Pour the peanut dressing over the salad and toss everything together until well coated.
4. Sprinkle chopped peanuts over the top of the salad for added crunch.
5. Serve the Thai Chicken and Peanut Salad with lime wedges on the side for squeezing over the salad before eating.
6. Enjoy your flavorful and satisfying Thai-inspired chicken and peanut salad!

Asparagus Chicken Salad

Prep time: 40 minutes | Cook time: none | Serves 4

Necessary products

1/4 cup Parmesan cheese
1/4 cup breadcrumbs
4 chicken breast halves, boneless and skinless
1 tablespoon olive oil
6 cups spinach leaves, stems removed
3 cups cooked rice
1 pound asparagus,
    blanched and cut into bite-sized pieces
2 tomatoes, sliced
1/2 cup leeks
1/3 cup walnuts, toasted
2/3 cup Vinaigrette salad dressing
Handful fresh parsley, roughly chopped

Preparation

1. In a medium bowl, combine cheese with breadcrumbs. Coat chicken breasts with this mixture.
2. Heat olive oil in a wide saucepan over medium-high heat. Fry chicken until browned. Transfer the chicken to the large bowl and set aside.
3. Add spinach, rice, asparagus, tomatoes, leeks, and walnuts. Toss to combine. Pour Vinaigrette salad dressing over salad just before serving and serve chilled.

Minty Green Chicken Salad

Prep time: 25 minutes | Cook time: 14 minutes |Serves 4

Necessary products

1 chicken breast, cubed
1 tbsp avocado oil
2 eggs
2 cups green beans, steamed
1 avocado, sliced
4 cups mixed salad greens
2 tbsp olive oil
2 tbsp lemon juice
1 tsp Dijon mustard
1 tbsp mint, chopped
Salt and black pepper to taste

Preparation

1. Boil the eggs in salted water over medium heat for 10 minutes. Remove to an ice bath to cool, peel and slice. Warm the oil in a pan over medium heat. Add the chicken and cook for about 4 minutes.
2. Divide the green beans between two salad bowls. Top with chicken, eggs, and avocado slices.
3. In another bowl, whisk together the lemon juice, olive oil, mustard, salt, and pepper, and drizzle over the salad. Top with mint and serve.

Pineapple, Cashew, and Chicken Salad

Prep time: 15 minutes | Cook time: 10 minutes | Serves 4

Necessary products
1 cup quinoa
½ pound chicken breast
Salt
Freshly ground black pepper
2 tablespoons coconut oil
1 cup diced pineapple
½ cup cashews
1 cup baby spinach
6 tablespoons Coconut-Lime Dressing

Preparation
1. Cook quinoa as per instructions. Fluff with a fork.
2. Season and cook the chicken in coconut oil. Slice into bite-size pieces.
3. Divide quinoa, chicken, pineapple, cashews, and spinach among four bowls. Drizzle with Coconut-Lime Dressing. Serve and enjoy the tropical flavors.

Mango Avocado Chicken Salad

Prep time: 25 minutes | Cook time: 15 minutes |Serves 4

Necessary products
2 cups cooked chicken breast, diced or shredded
1 ripe mango, peeled, pitted, and diced
1 ripe avocado, peeled, pitted, and diced
1/4 cup red onion, finely chopped
1/4 cup fresh cilantro, chopped
Juice of 1 lime
2 tablespoons mayonnaise
2 tablespoons Greek yogurt
Salt and pepper to taste
Lettuce leaves or mixed greens, for serving
Optional: sliced almonds or chopped walnuts for garnish

Preparation
1. In a large mixing bowl, combine the diced or shredded chicken breast, diced mango, diced avocado, chopped red onion, and chopped cilantro.
2. In a small bowl, whisk together the lime juice, mayonnaise, and Greek yogurt until smooth.
3. Pour the dressing over the chicken mixture and gently toss until everything is evenly coated.
4. Season the chicken salad with salt and pepper to taste. Adjust the seasoning as needed.
5. To serve, arrange lettuce leaves or mixed greens on a serving platter or individual plates.
6. Spoon the mango avocado chicken salad onto the lettuce leaves.
7. If desired, sprinkle sliced almonds or chopped walnuts over the top for added crunch and flavor.
8. Enjoy your refreshing mango avocado chicken salad!

Strawberry and Chicken Salad

Prep time: 20 minutes | Cook time: 5 minutes | Serves 3

Necessary products

For the Salad:
1 lb boneless, skinless chicken breasts, grilled or cooked and sliced
6 cups mixed salad greens (such as spinach, arugula, or mixed baby greens)
2 cups fresh strawberries, hulled and sliced
1/2 cup red onion, thinly sliced
1/2 cup feta cheese, crumbled
1/4 cup sliced almonds, toasted

For the Strawberry Vinaigrette:
1 cup fresh strawberries, hulled and halved
3 tablespoons balsamic vinegar
2 tablespoons honey or maple syrup
1/4 cup extra-virgin olive oil
Salt and pepper to taste

Preparation

1. In a large salad bowl, combine the mixed salad greens, sliced grilled chicken, sliced strawberries, red onion, crumbled feta cheese, and toasted sliced almonds.
2. In a blender or food processor, combine the halved strawberries, balsamic vinegar, honey or maple syrup, and a pinch of salt and pepper.
3. Blend until smooth, gradually adding the olive oil until the dressing is well combined.
4. Taste the dressing and adjust the sweetness or acidity if needed, adding more honey or balsamic vinegar accordingly.
5. Drizzle the strawberry vinaigrette over the salad.
6. Toss the salad gently to ensure all ingredients are well coated with the dressing.
7. Serve the Strawberry and Chicken Salad immediately, garnished with additional sliced strawberries or almonds if desired.

Mango, Avocado, and Chicken Salad

Prep time: 15 minutes | Cook time: 10 minutes | Serves 4

Necessary products
1 cup quinoa
½ pound chicken breast
Salt
Freshly ground black pepper
2 tablespoons olive oil
1 medium ripe mango, diced
1 large avocado, diced
1 cup cherry tomatoes, halved
6 tablespoons Lime-Cilantro Vinaigrette

Preparation
1. Cook the quinoa according to package instructions. Fluff with a fork.
2. Season the chicken with salt and pepper. Heat olive oil in a skillet and cook the chicken until done. Slice into bite-size pieces.
3. Divide quinoa and chicken among four bowls. Top with mango, avocado, and cherry tomatoes. Drizzle with Lime-Cilantro Vinaigrette. Serve and enjoy.

Chapter 8:

Savory Meat Salads

Fennel, Seared Pork, and Pineapple Salad

Prep time: 30 minutes | Cook time: 5 minutes | Serves 4

Necessary products

1 pound pork tenderloin, trimmed, de-
 boned (or purchase already de-boned),
 and cut into 12 (¼-inch) slices
Salt
Freshly ground black pepper
¼ cup grapeseed, vegetable, or canola oil
2 small fennel bulbs, fronds removed
½ cup Date-Balsamic Vinaigrette
½ small pineapple, diced (about 2 cups)

Preparation

1. Generously season the pork slices on both
    sides with salt and pepper.
2. Heat the oil in a large skillet over medium-high heat.
    When the oil is hot, add the pork slices in a single layer and sear them, about 3 minutes
    on each side. Cook in two batches, if necessary, or cook in two separate skillets to save
    time. Transfer the pork to a plate and let rest for 5 to 10 minutes.
3. While the pork rests, use a mandoline or very sharp knife to shave the fennel. Place it in
    a medium bowl and toss with the vinaigrette. Add the pineapple and toss to combine.
    Divide the fennel and pineapple among four bowls.
4. Slice the pork into thin strips. Top the salads with the pork strips and serve.

Asian-Style Steak Salad

Prep time: 5 minutes | Cook time:15 minutes | Servin 5

Necessary products

1 ½ pounds beef sirloin steaks,
sliced into bite-sized strips
1 ½ tablespoons fresh lemon juice
2 tablespoons soy sauce
2 bell peppers, sliced
2 tomatoes, sliced

Preparation

1. Heat up a wok that is previously greased
    with nonstick spray.
2. Once hot, fry the beef sirloin steaks for
    6 to 7 minutes, stirring and shaking the
    wok to ensure even cooking. Transfer to
    a nice salad bowl.
3. Toss with the lemon juice, soy sauce,
    bell peppers, and tomatoes and serve at
    room temperature. Enjoy!

Lamb and Greek Salad

Prep time: 20 minutes | Cook time: 15 minutes | Serves 4

Necessary products
1 pound lamb chops or lamb gyro slices
Salt and pepper
2 tablespoons olive oil
4 cups chopped romaine lettuce
1 cucumber, diced
1 cup cherry tomatoes, halved
½ cup Kalamata olives, pitted
½ cup crumbled feta cheese
6 tablespoons Greek Dressing

Preparation
1. Season lamb chops with salt and pepper. Grill or pan-sear until desired doneness. Slice into bite-size pieces.
2. Toss romaine lettuce, diced cucumber, cherry tomatoes, Kalamata olives, and crumbled feta cheese in a large bowl.
3. Top the salad with sliced lamb and drizzle with Greek Dressing. Toss gently and serve.

Easy Steak Salad

Prep time: 5 minutes | Cook time: 20 minutes | Serves 4

Necessary products
2 tablespoons olive oil
8 ounces flank steak, salt-and-pepper-seasoned
1 cucumber, sliced
1/2 cup onions, finely sliced
1 ripe avocado, peeled and sliced
2 medium-sized heirloom tomatoes, sliced
2 ounces baby arugula
1 tablespoon fresh coriander, chopped
3 tablespoons lime juice

Preparation
1. Heat 1 tablespoon of olive oil in a pan over medium-high heat. Cook the flank steak for 5 minutes, turning once or twice.
2. Let stand for 10 minutes; then, slice thinly across the grain. Transfer the meat to a bowl.
3. Add cucumbers, shallots, avocado, tomatoes, baby arugula, and fresh coriander. Now, drizzle your salad with lime juice and the remaining 1 tablespoon of olive oil.
4. Serve well chilled and enjoy!

BBQ Chicken and Corn Salad

Prep time: 20 minutes | Cook time: 15 minutes | Serves 4

Necessary products

1 pound boneless, skinless chicken breasts
Salt and pepper
½ cup barbecue sauce
2 cups corn kernels, grilled or roasted
1 red bell pepper, diced
1 cup black beans, drained and rinsed
6 cups mixed salad greens
6 tablespoons Ranch dressing

Preparation

1. Season chicken with salt and pepper. Grill and brush with barbecue sauce until fully cooked. Slice into strips.
2. In a large bowl, combine grilled corn, diced red bell pepper, black beans, mixed salad greens, and sliced barbecue chicken.
3. Drizzle with Ranch dressing, toss to coat, and serve.

Thai Beef Salad

Prep time: 20 minutes | Cook time: 10 minutes | Serves 4

Necessary products

1 pound flank steak
Salt and pepper
2 tablespoons soy sauce
2 tablespoons lime juice
1 tablespoon fish sauce
1 tablespoon brown sugar
2 cups mixed salad greens
1 cucumber, sliced
1 red onion, thinly sliced
½ cup chopped fresh cilantro

Preparation

1. Season the flank steak with salt and pepper. Grill or pan-sear until desired doneness, then slice thinly.
2. In a bowl, whisk together soy sauce, lime juice, fish sauce, and brown sugar.
3. Toss mixed greens, cucumber, red onion, and sliced steak in a large bowl. Drizzle with the dressing, sprinkle with cilantro, and serve.

Stuffed Pork with Red Cabbage Salad

Prep time: 40 minutes | Cook time: 27 minutes | Serves 4

Necessary products
Zest and juice from 2 limes
1 garlic cloves, minced
¾ cup olive oil
1 cup fresh cilantro, chopped
1 cup fresh mint, chopped
1 tsp dried oregano
Salt and black pepper, to taste
2 tsp cumin
4 pork loin steaks
2 pickles, chopped
4 ham slices
6 Swiss cheese slices
2 tbsp mustard
For The Salad
1   head red cabbage, shredded
2   tbsp vinegar
3   tbsp olive oilSalt to taste

Preparation
1. In a food processor, blitz the lime zest, oil, oregano, black pepper, cumin, cilantro, lime juice, garlic, mint, and salt. Rub the steaks with the mixture and toss well to coat; set aside for some hours in the fridge.
2. Arrange the steaks on a working surface, split the pickles, mustard, cheese, and ham on them, roll, and secure with toothpicks. Heat a pan over medium heat, add in the pork rolls, cook each side for 2 minutes and remove to a baking sheet. Bake in the oven at 350°F for 25 minutes. Prepare the red cabbage salad by mixing all salad ingredients and serve with the meat.

Taco Salad

Prep time: 30 minutes | Cook time: 5 minutes | Serves 4

Necessary products
1 tablespoon canola oil
1 pound ground beef
1½ teaspoons taco seasoning
8 cups shredded romaine lettuce
2 cups cherry tomatoes, halved
1 cup shredded Cheddar cheese
2 cups tortilla chips, roughly crumbled
¾ cup pitted black olives, sliced into rings (optional)
½ cup Roasted Poblano Crema

Preparation
1. Heat the oil in a large skillet over medium-high heat. Add the ground beef, mix in the taco seasoning, and cook, breaking the meat up with a wooden spoon, until fully browned and cooked through, about 6 minutes.
2. Arrange the salad on each of four plates. Begin with the romaine lettuce, then add the ground beef, tomatoes, and cheese, and top with the tortilla chips. Add the sliced black olives (if using). Drizzle with the poblano crema and serve warm.

Warm Rump Steak Salad

Prep time: 40 minutes | Cook time: 5 minutes | Serves 4

Necessary products
½ lb rump steak, excess fat trimmed
3 green onions, sliced
3 tomatoes, sliced
1 cup green beans, steamed and sliced
2 kohlrabi, peeled and chopped
½ cup water
2 cups mixed salad greens
Salt and black pepper to season
Salad Dressing
2 tsp Dijon mustard
1 tsp erythritol
Salt and black pepper to taste
3 tbsp olive oil + extra for drizzling
1 tbsp red wine vinegar

Preparation
1. Preheat the oven to 400°F. Place the kohlrabi on a baking sheet, drizzle with olive oil and bake in the oven for 25 minutes. After cooking, remove, and set aside to cool.
2. In a bowl, mix the Dijon mustard, erythritol, salt, black pepper, vinegar, and olive oil. Set aside.
3. Then, preheat a grill pan over high heat while you season the meat with salt and black pepper. Place the steak in the pan and brown on both sides for 4 minutes each. Remove to rest on a chopping board for 4 more minutes before slicing thinly.
4. In a salad bowl, add green onions, tomatoes, green beans, kohlrabi, salad greens, and steak slices. Drizzle the dressing over and toss with two spoons. Serve the steak salad warm with chunks of low carb bread.

Smoked Salmon and Asparagus Salad

Prep time: 15 minutes | Cook time: 10 minutes | Serves 3

Necessary products
8 ounces smoked salmon
1 bunch asparagus, trimmed and blanched
2 tablespoons capers
½ red onion, thinly sliced
6 cups arugula
6 tablespoons Dill-Citrus Vinaigrette

Preparation
1. Arrange smoked salmon, blanched asparagus, capers, red onion, and arugula on a serving platter.
2. Drizzle with Dill-Citrus Vinaigrette just before serving. Gently toss and enjoy this refreshing and flavorful smoked salmon and asparagus salad.

Thai Pork Salad

Necessary products

For the pork:
1 lb pork tenderloin, thinly sliced
2 tablespoons soy sauce
1 tablespoon fish sauce
1 tablespoon lime juice
1 tablespoon brown sugar
2 cloves garlic, minced
1 teaspoon grated ginger
1 tablespoon vegetable oil
For the salad:
4 cups mixed salad greens
(such as lettuce, cabbage, or spinach)
1 cucumber, thinly sliced
1 red onion, thinly sliced
1 bell pepper (any color), thinly sliced
1/4 cup fresh cilantro leaves
1/4 cup fresh mint leaves
1/4 cup roasted peanuts, chopped
For the dressing:
2 tablespoons lime juice
1 tablespoon fish sauce
1 tablespoon brown sugar
1 teaspoon chili flakes (adjust to taste)
1 clove garlic, minced

Preparation

1. In a bowl, whisk together the soy sauce, fish sauce, lime juice, brown sugar, minced garlic, and grated ginger to make the marinade.
2. Add the sliced pork to the marinade and toss to coat evenly. Let it marinate for at least 30 minutes, or up to 2 hours in the refrigerator.
3. Heat the vegetable oil in a skillet over medium-high heat. Add the marinated pork slices and cook for 2-3 minutes on each side, or until cooked through and nicely browned. Remove from heat and set aside.
4. In a large salad bowl, combine the mixed salad greens, sliced cucumber, sliced red onion, sliced bell pepper, cilantro leaves, and mint leaves.
5. In a small bowl, whisk together the lime juice, fish sauce, brown sugar, chili flakes, and minced garlic to make the dressing.
6. Add the cooked pork slices to the salad bowl.
7. Drizzle the dressing over the salad and toss gently to coat everything evenly.
8. Sprinkle chopped roasted peanuts over the salad for garnish.
9. Serve the Thai pork salad immediately and enjoy!

Turkey and Cranberry Quinoa Salad

Necessary products

1 cup quinoa
1 pound turkey breast, cooked and sliced
Salt and pepper
1 cup dried cranberries
½ cup feta cheese, crumbled
6 cups baby spinach
6 tablespoons Cranberry Vinaigrette

Preparation

1. Cook quinoa according to package instructions. Fluff with a fork.
2. Season turkey slices with salt and pepper.
3. In a large bowl, combine quinoa, turkey, dried cranberries, feta cheese, and baby spinach. Drizzle with Cranberry Vinaigrette and toss to combine. Serve and enjoy.

Beef and Feta Salad

Necessary products

3 tbsp olive oil
½ pound beef rump steak, cut into strips
Salt and black pepper, to taste
1 tsp cumin
A pinch of dried thyme 2 garlic cloves, minced
4 ounces feta cheese, crumbled
½ cup pecans, toasted
2 cups spinach
1½ tbsp lemon juice
¼ cup fresh mint, chopped

Preparation

1. Season the beef with salt, 1 tbsp of olive oil, garlic, thyme, pepper, and cumin. Place on a preheated to medium heat grill, and cook for 10 minutes, flip once. Remove the grilled beef to a cutting board, leave to cool, and slice into strips.
2. Sprinkle the pecans on a lined baking sheet, place in the oven at 350°F, and toast for 10 minutes. In a salad bowl, combine the spinach with black pepper, mint, remaining olive oil, salt, lemon juice, feta cheese, and pecans, and toss well to coat. Top with the beef slices and enjoy.

Grilled Steak and Blue Cheese Salad

Prep time: 15 minutes | Cook time: 10 minutes | Serves 4

Necessary products
1 pound sirloin steak
Salt and pepper
2 tablespoons olive oil
8 cups mixed greens
1 cup cherry tomatoes, halved
½ cup crumbled blue cheese
6 tablespoons Balsamic Vinaigrette

Preparation
1. Season the steak with salt and pepper. Grill to your preferred doneness, then slice thinly.
2. Toss mixed greens, cherry tomatoes, and sliced steak in a large bowl.
3. Sprinkle crumbled blue cheese over the top and drizzle with Balsamic Vinaigrette. Serve and enjoy.

Grilled Lamb and Mediterranean Couscous Salad

Prep time: 20 minutes | Cook time: 15 minutes | Serves 4

Necessary products
1 cup couscous
1.5 pounds lamb loin chops, grilled to medium and sliced
Salt and pepper
1 cup cucumber, diced
1 cup cherry tomatoes, halved
1/2 cup red bell pepper, finely chopped
1/4 cup red onion, thinly sliced
1/4 cup Kalamata olives, pitted and sliced
6 cups mixed greens (arugula, spinach, or your choice)
6 tablespoons Lemon-Herb Vinaigrette

Preparation
1. Cook couscous according to package instructions. Fluff with a fork.
2. Season grilled lamb slices with salt and pepper.
3. In a large bowl, combine couscous, grilled lamb, diced cucumber, halved cherry tomatoes, finely chopped red bell pepper, sliced red onion, Kalamata olives, and mixed greens.
4. Drizzle with Lemon-Herb Vinaigrette and toss to combine.
5. Serve immediately for a delightful Grilled Lamb and Mediterranean Couscous Salad.

Beef and Avocado Quinoa Salad

Prep time: 20 minutes | Cook time: 15 minutes | Serves 4

Necessary products

1 cup quinoa
1 pound sirloin or flank steak, cooked and thinly sliced
Salt and pepper
1 large avocado, diced
1/2 cup cherry tomatoes, halved
1/4 cup red onion, finely chopped
6 cups mixed salad greens
6 tablespoons Balsamic-Beef Vinaigrette

Preparation

1. Cook quinoa according to package instructions. Fluff with a fork.
2. Season the cooked and sliced beef with salt and pepper.
3. In a large bowl, combine quinoa, sliced beef, diced avocado, halved cherry tomatoes, finely chopped red onion, and mixed salad greens.
4. Drizzle with Balsamic-Beef Vinaigrette and toss to combine.
5. Serve immediately for a delicious Beef and Avocado Quinoa Salad. Enjoy!

MEASUREMENT CONVERSION CHART

VOLUME EQUIVALENTS(DRY)

US STANDARD	METRIC (APPROXIMATE)
1/8 teaspoon	0.5 mL
1/4 teaspoon	1 mL
1/2 teaspoon	2 mL
3/4 teaspoon	4 mL
1 teaspoon	5 mL
1 tablespoon	15 mL
1/4 cup	59 mL
1/2 cup	118 mL
3/4 cup	177 mL
1 cup	235 mL
2 cups	475 mL
3 cups	700 mL
4 cups	1 L

VOLUME EQUIVALENTS(LIQUID)

US STANDARD	US STANDARD (OUNCES)	METRIC (APPROXIMATE)
2 tablespoons	1 fl.oz.	30 mL
1/4 cup	2 fl.oz.	60 mL
1/2 cup	4 fl.oz.	120 mL
1 cup	8 fl.oz.	240 mL
1 1/2 cup	12 fl.oz.	355 mL
2 cups or 1 pint	16 fl.oz.	475 mL
4 cups or 1 quart	32 fl.oz.	1 L
1 gallon	128 fl.oz.	4 L

TEMPERATURES EQUIVALENTS

FAHRENHEIT(F)	CELSIUS(C) (APPROXIMATE)
225 °F	107 °C
250 °F	120 °C
275 °F	135 °C
300 °F	150 °C
325 °F	160 °C
350 °F	180 °C
375 °F	190 °C
400 °F	205 °C
425 °F	220 °C
450 °F	235 °C
475 °F	245 °C
500 °F	260 °C

WEIGHT EQUIVALENTS

US STANDARD	METRIC (APPROXIMATE)
1 ounce	28 g
2 ounces	57 g
5 ounces	142 g
10 ounces	284 g
15 ounces	425 g
16 ounces (1 pound)	455 g
1.5 pounds	680 g
2 pounds	907 g

Appendix 2: The Dirty Dozen and Clean Fifteen

The Dirty Dozen and Clean Fifteen

The Environmental Working Group (EWG) is a nonprofit, nonpartisan organization dedicated to protecting human health and the environment Its mission is to empower people to live healthier lives in a healthier environment. This organization publishes an annual list of the twelve kinds of produce, in sequence, that have the highest amount of pesticide residue-the Dirty Dozen-as well as a list of the fifteen kinds ofproduce that have the least amount of pesticide residue-the Clean Fifteen.

THE DIRTY DOZEN	THE CLEAN FIFTEEN
• The 2016 Dirty Dozen includes the following produce. These are considered among the year's most important produce to buy organic:	• The least critical to buy organically are the Clean Fifteen list. The following are on the 2016 list:

Strawberries	Spinach
Apples	Tomatoes
Nectarines	Bell peppers
Peaches	Cherry tomatoes
Celery	Cucumbers
Grapes	Kale/collard greens
Cherries	Hot peppers

Avocados	
Corn	Papayas
Pineapples	Kiw Eggplant
Cabbage	Honeydew
Sweet peas	Grapefruit
Onions	Cantaloupe
Asparagus	Cauliflower
Mangos	

The Dirty Dozen list contains two additional itemskale/collard greens and hot peppers-because they tend to contain trace levels of highly hazardous pesticides.

Some of the sweet corn sold in the United States are made from genetically engineered (GE) seedstock. Buy organic varieties of these crops to avoid GE produce.

Appendix 3: Index

A

almonds 36
apple 9, 16, 18, 46
apple cider vinegar 13, 18, 47
arugula 46
asparagus 49
avocado 9, 10, 15, 26, 32, 42, 44, 52, 62

B

baby spinach 50
bacon 28, 32
bag mixed green 35
bags shaved 13
balsamic 19
balsamic vinegar 24, 28, 40, 51
barbecue sauce 56
basil 42
basil pesto 15
beans 29
bell pepper 22, 48
black beans 24, 56
blackberries 14
black olive 21
black pepper 57, 58
blueberries 14
boneless 48, 51
box coconut shrimp 35
breadcrumbs 49
broccoli florets 47
brown rice vinegar 21
brown sugar 19, 25, 56

C

cabbage 35
canned tuna 36
canola oil 13, 57
capers 58
capsicum 8
carrots 19, 37
cashews 50
cauliflower 18
cayenne pepper 18, 41, 42
celery 35, 37
celery stalk 45
cheese 49
cherry tomatoe 35, 45, 47, 62
cherry tomatoes 38, 39, 52, 61
chicken 45, 47

chicken breast 45, 46, 47, 50, 52
chicken breast halves 49
chickpeas 24
chilli pepper 16
chives 14
chopped fresh cilantro 56
chopped snap peas 25
chopped walnuts 46
cilantro 21, 22, 57
cilantro leave 10
cinnamon 11
cleaned 18, 23
clove garlic 9, 25, 38, 48
cloves garlic 9, 28, 37, 40, 42
Coconut-Lime Dressing 50
coconut oil 50
cooked beans 24
cooked black 22
cooked rice 49
cored 13, 18, 19
corn 17, 26, 41, 44, 56
couscous 61
creamy peanut butter 48
Creole mustard 40
crumbled blue cheese 61
cucumber 37, 39, 47, 48, 55, 61
cumin 11, 57
cups mixed salad 56
curry powder 30

D

dates 9
diced pineapple 50
Dijon mustard 22, 28, 38, 45
dill sprig 7
dried thyme 19

E

egg 23, 28, 30, 31, 32, 33, 38
erythritol 58
extra-virgin olive oil 7, 22, 32, 33, 35, 38, 41, 47, 51

F

fennel bulbs 54
feta 55
feta cheese 22, 36, 51
finely 24

finely chopped 28
finely sliced 16
fish 37
fish sauce 56
flank steak 56
flowers 40
fresh basil 9
fresh basil leave 33
fresh cilantro 25, 26, 32, 41, 48
fresh cilantro leave 7, 11
fresh dill 39, 42
fresh finely 16
fresh ginger 25, 48
fresh lemon 39, 41
fresh lemon juice 9, 15, 33
freshly ground black pepper 18, 28
freshly squeezed 22
freshly squeezed lime juice 17, 35, 41, 44
fresh mint 57
fresh mint leave 8
fresh mint leaves 25, 48
fresh mozzarella 33
fresh parsley 35, 39
fresh strawberries 51
frozen precooked shrimp 41

G

garlic clove 7, 8, 10, 22
garlic cloves 21, 24, 57
garlic powder 19
golden raisins 18
grapeseed oil 7
grape tomatoe 32
grape tomatoes 21
grated 11
Greek Dressing 55
greek yogurt 30
Greek yogurt 8, 10
green bean 58
green beans 21, 38
green onion 40
green onions 25, 30, 58
ground beef 57
ground black pepper 7, 8, 10, 15, 19, 23, 24,
    40, 42, 46, 47, 50, 52, 54
ground cayenne pepper 17
ground cumin 8, 26, 41

H

hazelnuts 18
honey 9, 11, 23, 25, 26, 28, 35, 39, 48, 51

J

juiced 26
julienned 19, 25, 29, 48

K

kidney beans 24
kosher salt 22, 23, 35, 41, 44

L

lamb chops 55
leaves separated 23
lemon 7, 8, 22, 23
lemon juice 10, 28, 32, 36, 40, 42, 44
Lemon juice 29
lemon zest 18, 24
lettuce 41
lettuce leave 37, 42
lime juice 31, 32, 36, 56
limes 7
long-grain rice 24
low-sodium soy sauce 11

M

mango 9
mango chutney 30
Mangoes 31
mayonnaise 17, 23, 32, 35, 36, 40, 41, 42,
    44, 45
minced chives 11
mixed 58
mixed greens 16, 46, 61
mixed salad greens 38, 51, 56, 62
Mixed salad greens 29, 30

O

olive 11, 29, 36, 55
olive oil 8, 9, 10, 13, 14, 15, 18, 21, 23, 26, 31,
    33, 36, 39, 40, 47, 49, 52, 55, 57, 58,
    61
Olive oil 29
onion 29, 35, 36, 37, 45
onion powder 19
onions 13
orange juice 10, 19, 25
orange zest 11
oregano 9, 57
orzo pasta 22
oysters 41

P

paprika 9, 17, 42, 44
parsley 14
parsley leave 10
peanuts 48
pecan oil 46
peeled 13, 14, 21, 22, 25, 36, 58
pepper 21, 22, 24, 25, 26, 33, 41, 55, 56, 60
peppers 33
pepper to taste 31
pickles 37, 57
pineapple salsa 35
pitted black olives 57
pork loin 57
potatoes 38
pound sirloin 62
premade broccoli slaw mix 25
prepared horseradish 42
pure maple syrup 18

Q

quinoa 39, 46, 47, 50, 52, 60, 62

R

raspberries 10, 14
red bell pepper 47, 56, 61
red cabbage 13
red chilli 8
red onion 17, 18, 22, 25, 26, 32, 39, 44, 51,
          58, 61, 62
Red onion 31
red pepper 14
red pepper flakes 35
red potatoes 14
red wine vinegar 11, 26, 38, 45
rice noodle 25
rice noodles 48
rice vinegar 25, 48
rice wine vinegar 19, 25
ripe mango 52
romaine lettuce 17, 36, 44, 45, 55, 57
rotisserie chicken 44
rump steak 58

S

salad dressing to taste 35
salmon 37, 42
salt 7, 8, 14, 17, 42
scallions 33, 41
sea salt 11, 28, 40

S

sea scallop 39
sesame oil 11, 25, 48
sesame seeds 19, 25
shawarma seasoning 45
shelled edamame 25
shredded cabbage 48
shrimp 39, 42
sirloin steak 61
sliced 47, 49
slivered 13
sour cream 7, 17
soy sauce 19, 25, 48, 56
spinach leave 49
sprouts 19
strawberries 14
sweet paprika 40

T

taco seasoning 57
tarragon leave 40
taste 18, 24
thinly sliced 29, 46
thyme leave 42
toasted pecans 46
tofu block 33
tomatoe 33, 36, 47, 58
tomatoes 8, 9, 15, 17, 21, 24, 29, 55, 57
tortilla chips 57
trimmed 36, 54
tuna fish 35
turkey breast 60

V

vegetable 54
vegetable oil 13, 19, 25

W

walnut oil 46
walnuts 18, 19
water 18, 48, 58
white vinegar 23
white wine vinegar 21

X

xtra-virgin olive oil 45

Y

yellow mustard 23, 37

Z

zucchinis 15

Printed in Great Britain
by Amazon

44903245R00044